"*Momnipotent* offers practical and h
herself in the trenches of domestic
openly address the issues that every motner struggies with, even if no one wants
to admit to it! If you sometimes question your own sanity as a mom, read this
book and you'll find comfort in knowing you're not alone."

—**Crystalina Evert**
Speaker, author, and founder of *Women Made New*

"*Momnipotent* isn't just a book for moms. It's a book for every woman. No matter
what your station in life, in the pages of Danielle Bean's book, you'll see yourself—
your struggles, your fears, your insecurities, and your desires. You'll find wise
guidance for overcoming those struggles, realizing those desires, and becoming
the woman God made you to be."

—**Emily Stimpson**
Author of *These Beautiful Bones: An Everyday Theology of the Body*

"Danielle Bean's *Momnipotent* unpacks true-to-life wisdom for wives and mothers
as it showcases the feminine genius. With wit and honesty, Bean explores eight
great womanly strengths, as well as a recovery plan if those gifts are ignored or
misused. *Momnipotent* encourages and inspires us to consider why 'Mom' really
is 'Wow' spelled upside down!"

—**Pat Gohn,** author of *Blessed, Beautiful,* and
Bodacious: Celebrating the Gift of Catholic Womanhood

"Danielle Bean's *Momnipotent* is the perfect combination of empathy,
encouragement, and insight to uplift every mother—and those who love with a
mother's heart. By approaching motherhood as a vocation (and not just a path
to self-fulfillment), Danielle helps moms to understand themselves as ministers
to their families in a unique and profound way. She reminds us all that we were
created for motherhood and inspires us to approach this vital role in faithful
recognition that it is a gift from God for us and for those we love. When you're
feeling overwhelmed, unsatisfied, exhausted, fat, and unappreciated, take the
time to read *Momnipotent* ... and remember the power of a mother's love."

—**Marybeth Hicks,** weekly columnist for the *The Washington Times* and
Founder and editor of OntheCulture.com

"In true Danielle Bean fashion, this book is a balm for the weary mother's soul. It will bring hope and encouragement to any mom who has ever uttered the words, 'I can't do this.'"

—Hallie Lord
Editor and contributing author of *Style, Sex, and Substance: 10 Catholic Women Consider the Things that Really Matter*

"*Momnipotent* is reality meets compassion for moms of all stripes. You'll feel like your best friend is sitting across from you at the kitchen table, sharing a cup of your favorite hot beverage, and you'll come away changed and heartened from reading this book. Danielle Bean has taken the best of her experience as a mom of many, topped it with a hearty dose of John Paul II, and finished it with a smile and a hug. Be warned, though. You're going to want to keep this book, so you had better plan on buying a copy for your best friend!"

—Sarah Reinhard, author of *A Catholic Mother's Companion to Pregnancy: Walking with Mary from Conception to Baptism* and SnoringScholar.com

"Danielle Bean is every mom's mentor, soul sister, and cheerleader because she understands not only the challenges, but also the great graces, of being a mom. *Momnipotent* will help you move to the next level in your vocation by empowering you with feminine strengths for your vocation. Whether you're a new mom, a seasoned veteran, or even a spiritual mother, this book will be a true blessing for you and your family."

—Lisa Hendey
Founder of CatholicMom.com and author of *The Grace of Yes*

MOMNIPOTENT

The Not-So-Perfect Woman's Guide to Catholic Motherhood

DANIELLE BEAN

ASCENSION
West Chester, Pennsylvania

Nihil obstat: Rev. Msgr. Joseph G. Prior, S.S.L., S.T.D.
           Censor Librorum
           December 10, 2013

Imprimatur: +Most Reverend Charles J. Chaput, O.F.M. Cap.
           Archbishop of Philadelphia
           December 17, 2013

Ascension
Post Office Box 1990
West Chester, PA 19380
1-800-376-0520
ascensionpress.com

Cover design: Devin Schadt

Printed in the United States of America
19 20 21 22 23 6 5 4 3 2

ISBN 978-1-935940-61-6

To Mary, our mother in heaven,
who personifies feminine beauty, grace, and strength,
and who lovingly guides each of us
as we discover our own.

Contents

Acknowledgments

No mom is an island. This book came to fruition because of the inspiration, hard work, and dedication of many people. In particular, I would like to thank Matthew Pinto, president of Ascension Press, for believing in the dignity and worth of every woman, for having a heart for struggling moms, and for calling me from out of the blue and offering me the opportunity to write a book just for them. I am deeply grateful to Ascension's Theology of the Body director, Steve Motyl, who listened patiently through my anxious phone calls, reassured me when I thought all might be lost, and continually inspired me to give this project my all.

I would also like to thank Claudia Volkman and Heidi Saxton, who lent their editorial talents to this work and kept it moving toward completion, and the many talented people at Ascension whose gifts and talents helped bring this book to press, including: Chris Cope, Mike Fontecchio, Lora Brecker, Stella Ziegler, Chris Michalski, Kate Camden, and Mike Flickinger.

I am grateful to my mom, my sisters, and all the beautiful women I am blessed to call friends who listened to me as I worked out the themes of the book, let me pick their brains, and shared their humor, vulnerabilities, wisdom, and joy, as only fellow women can. I am especially grateful to my dear friend Tiffany, who read an early draft of the book during a time of critical transition and generously offered honest and helpful feedback.

Of course, I must thank my children—Kateri, Eamon, Ambrose, Juliette, Stephen, Gabrielle, Raphael, and Daniel—for continually asking if I was "done writing that best seller" yet and for their unfailing love, patience, and forgiveness as I figure this mom thing out. They are the ones who make me "momnipotent" and remind me if ever I forget I am.

And finally, I want to thank my husband, Dan. Every day God gives me the grace I need to do his will, and every day that grace comes to me through Dan. He gave up many date nights and weekend afternoons to hold down the fort while I worked for hours behind a locked door. He never complained or failed to "interrupt" at just the right time with a glass of wine. He believes in me more than I believe in myself, and without his confidence, words of encouragement, and behind the scenes support, this book would never have been possible. I love you, Dan. Thank God for you.

"To be feminine is to be expansive."

–St. Teresa Benedicta of the Cross

Introduction

"This is my little piece of happiness," my friend told me as she sat in her living room and nursed her infant son. "Right here, holding this baby and taking care of him."

Her beaming face told me she was speaking the truth, and I marveled at the peaceful scene.

What made her so content with something seemingly so small? Was she still basking in a postpartum hormonal glow? Had she managed to sleep three consecutive hours the previous night and was now riding high until the next crashing wave of fatigue?

Maybe.

But maybe her contentment was real. Maybe she was experiencing the kind of natural joy and contentment God intends every woman to find in motherhood.

And yet so few of us do—at least on any type of consistent basis.

Standing there, watching my friend exude pure joy as she fed her son in a small corner of her cluttered living room, I felt a sudden urge to capture some of her "mom-bliss" and bottle it. It certainly would be a handy remedy to prescribe in hefty doses for the young moms, old moms, poor moms, harried moms, and moms from all walks of life from whom I hear every day. I would love to prescribe a "happy-mother" pill to all the hurting women who reach out to me with heartrending tales of their interior struggles with finding joy in motherhood.

So many of us struggle.

I have a special place in my heart for moms who struggle. I have been the blissful mom, floating away on heart-shaped clouds and fluffy, sweet-scented diapers, but I have also been the disillusioned mom, tired and angry, because all she sees or smells is the mess.

A little more than ten years ago, my husband was working extra hours at a second job. I had a cranky, teething baby with an aversion to naps and an impending eye infection. I had a potty-training two-year-old who was solely responsible for a befouled area rug, a damp sofa cushion, and a full load of laundry washed, dried, folded, put away ... and soiled again.

As if all of this were not enough, next came a crash from the kitchen, where my four-year-old was attempting to pour herself a glass of Kool-Aid.

A mother simply does not ignore crashes of this kind, and so I did what a mother must do. I stepped over piles of unfolded laundry and made my way with haste to the scene where I found my wide-eyed, pigtailed daughter standing on a chair by the counter, blinking back tears and biting her lower lip. The kitchen tiles were spattered with orange Kool-Aid and shards of broken glass.

I sighed, grabbed a nearby dish towel, clenched my jaw, and stooped to mop up the sticky mess. Warily, my daughter stepped down from her chair and stood beside me in silence. I knew she wanted me to tell her it was OK, but I could not bring myself to do it.

It was not OK. I was exhausted, and this accident felt like one mess too many.

I avoided her eyes and wiped the floor harder still. I did not realize that I had cut my hand until I saw the blood. It trickled from my fingers and dribbled onto the floor, mixing with orange Kool-Aid. Quickly, I wrapped my fist in the towel. As I sat bleeding on the floor, tears of frustration stung at my eyes.

"I can't do this," I heard myself mutter. The words came out of my mouth before I even knew what I was saying, and the fact that I truly felt incapable startled me. *Was* I capable of being a good mom? Though I loved my children, I had to admit that, at the end of many days, I felt disillusioned, depleted, and perplexed by my own weakness and unhappiness.

The words on my lips were, "I can't do this," but deep inside were other words I dared not give voice to:

I am not happy. I hate this life. I want to give up.

I know I am not the only woman who has ever held such unhappy thoughts deep inside where they fester and burn, where they deplete her self-worth and wound her soul. And so often we feel we cannot speak our feelings aloud; what good would it do? Our husbands, good men that most of them are, often underestimate the nonstop, ever-present reality of work and sacrifice that make up the life of the seriously engaged mother. Sure, at times when our complaints reach a fevered pitch, they enter into our struggle—briefly—to lift our spirits in the moment. But much of the time, ours is a solitary struggle.

So this book is for unhappy, struggling moms. It is also for those of us who, in moments of restlessness, boredom, or the frustration of seeing other women who appear to "have it all," wonder if what we are doing now can legitimately be considered a life's work.

I want to bring good news to those who silently suffer—a life-giving message of joyful confidence and self-worth. And yet, this book is not my message. It is God's message, written on every woman's heart and made clear to us through the teachings of the Church and, in a special way, through the inspired words of St. John Paul II.

> As we contemplate this Mother, whose heart "a sword has pierced" (cf. Luke 2:35), our thoughts go to *all the suffering women in the world*, suffering either physically or morally. In this suffering a women's sensitivity plays a role, even though she often succeeds in resisting suffering better than a man. ... We may recall her maternal care for her children, especially when they fall sick or fall into bad ways; the death of those most dear to her; the loneliness of mothers forgotten by their grown-up children; the loneliness of widows; the sufferings of women who struggle alone to make a living; and women who have been wronged or exploited. ... These sufferings too we must place ourselves at the foot of the Cross.[1]

Of course, motherhood is not all about—or even primarily about—suffering. If you are in a particularly joyful season of life, this book is for you, too. In an often contrary world, we all need a reminder of the irreplaceable gift that we are to our families and, consequently, to society at large. We all need reassurance that our hidden work, done in the hearts of our homes, is life-changing, world-changing stuff that only we can do. We all need a reminder that the work we do as mothers does, in fact, matter. In fact, it matters more than many of

---

[1]   *Mulieris Dignitatem* 19.

us will ever know. We all need to be reminded of that special power we hold as women—our "momnipotence," if you will.

Momnipotence is a special charism that all moms have. Momnipotence is the special array of gifts given by God—lived out in particular through the vocation of motherhood—that blesses our families and the world. Gifts of love, gentleness, insight, compassion, and more enable us to live out to the fullest our role as spouse and mother. These gifts are both our call to greatness and the means by which we can help others, specifically our children, find their call to greatness.

Unlike the only being who is truly omnipotent—God—we moms certainly are not all-powerful. The proof of this is that we still overcook every fourth meal or bark at our kids at the end of a particularly tiring day. But, in the wisdom of that same God, we do possess a power that is unparalleled in society and, in particular, our families—the ability to love in unique and necessary ways. Every woman is "momnipotent," whether she knows it or not.

What Happy Mothers Know

The babies are the same. The diapers are the same. The laundry is the same. What makes one mom see the bliss and another mom see the mess? What makes one mom feel overwhelmed and another mom feel "momnipotent"? What makes one mom disgruntled—whether over the piles of laundry she returns to at night, or the piles that build up around her all day—and another hum to herself as she spins and folds? Why does the Church contend that *"the man* be fully aware that in their shared parenthood he owes *a special debt to the woman"*?[2] Let's find out.

---

[2]   *Mulieris Dignitatem* 18.

Chapter 1

What Women Can Be

"Thank you, every woman, for the simple fact of being a woman! Through the insight which is so much a part of your womanhood you enrich the world's understanding and help to make human relations more honest and authentic."

—Letter of St. John Paul II to Women

"The mystery of femininity is manifested and revealed completely by means of motherhood."

—St. John Paul II, General Audience, March 12, 1980

I will never forget the day I realized that *Sesame Street* had turned me into an angry woman. I was fifteen at the time.

Like many of my generation, I was raised with a healthy appreciation for all things *Sesame Street*. One night at dinner, when my parents and eight siblings and I were all seated at the family dinner table, a couple of my older brothers got a little goofy, poking fun at a popular *Sesame Street* song we all knew.

I knew the song they were singing. I knew it well. Perhaps you do too. It was called "Women Can Be" and featured Betty Lou, a charming little Muppet with blonde braids. Along with a crowd of older Muppet ladies, Betty Lou sang about the vast variety of career opportunities that were newly open to females.

The song described the "old" occupations of women and compared these to newer and ostensibly more exciting opportunities for women's careers. One lady who used to "sew dresses with needle and thread" became a brain surgeon instead. Another, who used to ride her bicycle around the block and make it home in time for dinner became an astronaut, flying her rocket to the moon. As the song continues, still more female Muppets describe their adventures as lumberjacks, truck drivers, and lion tamers.

The refrain is a catchy one:

Just look around you, it's easy to see ...
There's nothing we women can't be![1]

My brothers made fun of the *Sesame Street* song. "We can be priests and we can be popes!" they sang, laughing. They really did not intend to belittle female accomplishments. They were sarcastically pointing out the problematic thinking of those who believe there are no innate differences between the sexes and no limits to what women can do or be.

But the nuance was lost on me. Their jokes made me angry.

It's just a song, I remember thinking hotly. Who were they to make fun of the fact that modern women enjoy opportunities in

---

[1]   Carol Hall and Sam Pottle, *Women Can Be* (Sesame Street, Inc., 1974). http://muppet. wikia.com/wiki/Women_Can_Be.

previously male-dominated fields? The song did not say anything at all about a woman becoming a pope or priest!

I left the table in a huff. Then, sitting in my room silently stewing, I pondered a foreign feeling—an angry righteousness rising in my chest.

Where did that come from?

Saturated and Frustrated

Maybe I am being silly here, analyzing the lyrics of a *Sesame Street* jingle from the '70s. Perhaps this is just one little song—a harmless bit of feel-good, pro-woman, ego-boosting fun.

But I cannot help but recognize now something that I could only sense at the time: Something larger was at work, both in the lyrics and in my strong reaction.

The song is a microcosm of the culture in which many of us post-Baby Boomers grew up. It is a small but accurate taste of modern thought about the role of women that many of us, even those raised in traditional families, might never before have thought to question.

Though my teenaged self was not prepared to see it back then, my brothers' jokes correctly highlighted what was off-base in both the *Sesame Street* song and in much of the popular culture at that time.

"There's nothing we women can't be" is a smooth-sounding slogan, but is it true?

There might be nothing we women cannot do these days, but can we change who we *are?* Can we change the plan God has written on our hearts, minds, bodies, and souls? The fundamental question every woman must answer in her lifetime is not what she will be or what she will do, but *who she is.*

Who did God make me to be? Every woman's answer to that question, in one form or another, is "mother."

God Made Every Woman to Be a Mother

Does the boldness of those words make you uncomfortable? In some ways, it makes me uncomfortable to type them. This is because, in the name of female "empowerment," many of us have grown up in a cultural sea of anti-motherhood propaganda.

You simply do not tell women God made them to be mothers. You do not say that kind of thing. It is belittling and demeaning.

Really?

One of the fundamental tenets of modern popular thought is the rejection of traditional marriage and motherhood as cultural clichés that enslave women and rob them of their identities. Or so many would have us believe.

In our haste to convince the world that there is nothing we women cannot be, though, we run the risk of betraying the persons we actually are. When I say we are all called to be mothers, I recognize that not all of us will be biological mothers, or even adoptive mothers. I am speaking about motherhood in a much broader sense—a sense that can and does include religious sisters, single women, and women unable to have biological children. St. John Paul II described this concept beautifully in *Mulieris Dignitatem* ("On the Dignity and Vocation of Women").

Spiritual motherhood takes on many different forms. In the life of consecrated women, for example, who live according to the charism and the rules of the various apostolic Institutes, it can express itself as concern for people, especially the most needy: the sick, the handicapped, the abandoned, orphans, the elderly, children, young people, the imprisoned and, in general, people on the edges of society.[2]

This is a concept that Katrina Zeno expands upon in her book on spiritual motherhood, *Discovering the Feminine Genius,* when she writes:

It makes sense ... that while some women are called to biological motherhood, *every woman is called to spiritual motherhood because motherhood is knit into the very structure of a woman's being.* Women are created with the gift of interior readiness to receive others into their lives, and in doing so, to nurture their emotional, moral, cultural, and spiritual well-being. This is an exciting and creative challenge because women can be spiritual mothers anywhere: in the office, at home, with their grandchildren, in the neighborhood, even sick in bed.[3]

In this way, we can understand our common calling to motherhood as a womanly vocation to love, nurture, and care for the most needy among us. Those we care for might include biological children, adopted children, nieces, nephews, neighbors, students, patients, the disabled, the elderly, the poor, and any number of others in need of our love. Answering the womanly call to motherhood—to love—is a uniquely feminine privilege and responsibility.

---

[2]   *Mulieris Dignitatem* 21.
[3]   Katrina J. Zeno, *Discovering the Feminine Genius: Every Woman's Journey* (Boston: Pauline Books & Media, 2010), 41.

The special gifts and graces God gives us as mothers are part of what I like to call our "momnipotence," the kind of strength and power that belong uniquely to women. When we deny our call to motherhood and fail to recognize its intrinsic dignity and worth, we deny the very gifts that make us uniquely female. When we pretend that we are identical to men, we betray our feminine selves and reject our most important strengths.

Betraying authentic femininity and squashing our true nature as women does not sound very empowering to me. What does sound empowering is the term "feminine genius." John Paul II coined this phrase as a way of describing the unique and essential contributions women make to our families, our communities, and our Church.

> In fact, woman has a genius all her own, which is vitally essential to both society and the Church. It is certainly not a question of comparing woman to man, since it is obvious that they have fundamental dimensions and values in common. However, in man and in woman these acquire different strengths, interests, and emphases and it is this very diversity which becomes a source of enrichment.[4]

Motherhood Matters

I have no issue with women who want to become astronauts or lion tamers. But ... what about mothers?

It is no accident that there was no mention of motherhood as a legitimate and honorable female vocation in the alluring list of modern Muppet careers in "Women Can Be."

---

[4]   John Paul II, Angelus, 23 July 1995.

Not a word about the miraculous, heroic, self-giving love of a woman who conceives and carries new life within her own flesh. No mention of the kind of maternal generosity present in orders of religious women who nurture entire generations of children, poor, elderly, and infirm. None.

Every Woman's Calling

Motherhood is a privilege but also an inescapable part of every woman's calling. In a general audience given on January 10, 1979, Pope John Paul II said:

> Motherhood is woman's vocation. It is an eternal vocation, and it is also a contemporary vocation. "The Mother who understands everything and embraces each of us with her heart": these are words of a song, sung by young people in Poland, which come into my mind at this moment. The song goes on to announce that today the world is particularly "hungry and thirsty" for that motherhood, which is woman's vocation "physically" and "spiritually," as it is Mary's.

How does your heart respond to these bold words? Are you cringing at the pope's audacity in calling every woman to "motherhood" or smiling at his affirmation of your gifts? In her book, *The Church and the Culture War*, Joyce Little, a theology professor at the University of St. Thomas, says of this quotation:

> Nothing demonstrates more clearly the poisoned character of contemporary human and social values than the fact that this kind of statement is not only unappreciated by so many of us today but is actually ridiculed as trivializing the importance of women in the Church and in the world. Motherhood is seen in some circles today, and those circles seem to be expanding, as demeaning to women because it removes them to such an extent

from what is valued as really important, which is to say, the
conspicuous achievements in society.[5]

How sad. How true. We hear this kind of anti-motherhood
sentiment frequently in popular culture.

The morning after the then-very-pregnant Hollywood actress
Natalie Portman accepted an Oscar for Best Actress at the 2011
Academy Awards, *Salon.com* contributor Mary Elizabeth Williams
was furious. What was Ms. Portman's offense? Well, she referred
to motherhood as "the most important role" of her life.

> She was as lovely and slightly awkward ... thanking her fellow
> nominees, her parents, the directors who've guided her career,
> and then at last "my beautiful love," dancer and choreographer
> Benjamin Millepied, for giving her "the most important role of
> my life." That'd be when he impregnated her, I'd wager.

> At the time, the comment jarred me, as it does every time anyone
> refers to motherhood as *the most important thing* a woman can
> possibly do. ... When you're pregnant, especially for the first
> time, there are a lot of amazed and awed moments in between
> the heartburn and insomnia. But is motherhood really a greater
> role than being secretary of state or a justice on the Supreme
> Court? Is reproduction automatically the greatest thing Natalie
> Portman will do with her life?[6]

Well, the short answer to Ms. Williams' question would be, "Yes!
Motherhood is the most important role any woman ever plays on
earth." Not because women are reproductive machines, not because
women cannot excel at everything from achieving Hollywood

5   Joyce A. Little, *The Church and the Culture War: Secular Anarchy or Sacred Order* (San
    Francisco: Ignatius Press, 1995), 141.
6   Mary Elizabeth Williams, "Is Motherhood Natalie Portman's 'Greatest Role'?" Salon.com,
    February 28, 2011. http://www.salon.com/2011/02/28/natalie_portman_most_important_role/.

fame to serving on the Supreme Court, but because it is in our motherhood, in the reception and bearing of new life, that we reflect the creative power of God himself. This is a privileged role to play, one through which we achieve the most important things human beings can ever accomplish. If we ridicule and belittle the role of motherhood, the very place where women exercise their greatest strengths and find meaning and purpose for their greatest gifts, how can we expect happy and fulfilled individuals to result?

"Hey, what's the matter with you, modern woman?" Muppets and others might wonder. "How can you be unhappy when we've showered you with material goods, career opportunities, and public recognition for your professional achievements?"

Poor "modern woman." No wonder she is confused.

The Worth of a Woman

The Muppet song and the attitudes it represents might be well-intentioned, but they are shortsighted. St. John Paul II, on the other hand, heroically refuses to sell women short. In *Mulieris Dignitatem*, he notes that women are unique in their capacity to love and nurture other human beings, and that society owes us a debt for our feminine strength and generosity.

> *A woman is strong because of her awareness of this entrusting,* strong because of the fact that God "entrusts the human being to her," always and in every way, even in the situations of social discrimination in which she may find herself. This awareness and this fundamental vocation speak to women of the dignity which they receive from God himself, and this makes them "strong" and strengthens their vocation. Thus the "perfect woman" (cf. Proverbs 31:10) becomes an irreplaceable support

and source of spiritual strength for other people, who perceive
the great energies of her spirit. These "perfect women" are owed
much by their families, and sometimes by whole nations.[7]

It has been my observation, however, that even those of us who
do our best to embrace and honor our roles as mothers sometimes
suffer the residual effects of having been raised in a culture of
contrary thinking. There is sometimes a nagging feeling, an
unspoken thought, that motherhood is oppressive and that fully
engaging our feminine generosity will deplete us.

How can we find joy in giving our lives to little things—wiping
noses and scrubbing bathtubs—when there is some part, not only
in our culture, but also in the depths of our very hearts that rejects
the worth of our gift?

We need to look even deeper into our hearts with an open mind.
God has written a message there, a purpose for which we were
made, a plan that will bring us peace and joy, if only we will see
it. We find joy in the truth, however politically unpopular it might
be, and our experience of the truth begins with our senses, our
physical selves, and what we can know through our bodies.

Male and female God made us. We have different strengths and
different weaknesses. Women alone can be mothers, an inherently
dignified and worthy vocation, one in which we grow closer to
Christ and take part in the wonders of God's creation in real and
meaningful ways. Part of what I hope to accomplish in these pages
is an elucidation of this truth about women. We are going to talk
about those things that make up what St. John Paul II called our
"feminine genius"—a gift only we women have that we are meant

---

[7]   *Mulieris Dignitatem* 30.

to use in service to our families, our communities, and our Church. This gift is the stuff that "momnipotence" is made of.

Are you ready to learn more about your own momnipotence—your own unique gift of feminine, motherly strength? Let's take a closer look at the question: Do our lives, as "mere moms" have dignity? As we dispense fresh diapers, juice boxes, and taxi service, is it possible that we are literally changing the world with these mundane activities ... for the good?

One of the casualties of our failure to acknowledge our uniquely feminine characteristics is our own happiness. Women's uniquely feminine traits do not simply disappear if we fail to recognize and value them. When we lose sight of our uniquely female talents and gifts, we lose sight of God's plan for us. We risk using our gifts in an unbalanced or improper way, and we lose our way along the path toward lasting joy.

In the following chapters, we will look at some of our uniquely feminine gifts, and we will examine some of the ways in which these unique strengths can be expressed as weaknesses if we are not careful about the ways in which we use them. By finding balance and reflecting on some of our greatest feminine strengths along with making an honest assessment of our weaknesses and vulnerabilities, we can find real and lasting fulfillment in our God-given roles as mothers. We can grow closer to becoming the momnipotent women God created us to be.

No man will ever be a mother—even if he can do "motherly" things. In his very being, his ontological essence, he is always "father." He cannot be what God did not make him.

Likewise, we women can be only what God made us to be. This is not a weakness, but the very definition of our strength. Our greatest calling and dignity lies in what only we women can be. We recognize our fullest potential in giving others an authentic gift of ourselves. We discover the joy of the life God has planned for us through our vocation to motherhood.

Let's work on a positive, feminine, life-affirming response to our Muppet friends. We are women. We are momnipotent. There is so much we mothers can be.

Chapter 2

Beautiful Me, Beautiful You

"This world ... in which we live needs beauty in order not to sink into despair. Beauty, like truth, brings joy to the human heart and is that precious fruit which resists the erosion of time, which unites generations and enables them to be one in admiration!"

—Venerable Paul VI[1]

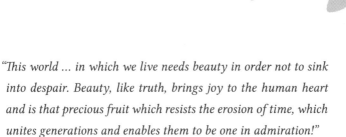

Strength:
We appreciate beauty.

Weakness:
We are vulnerable to materialism and envy.

---

[1] Message to Artists, 8 December 1965: AAS 58 (1966), 13.

I am not sure just how it happened, but I think I missed my "glory years."

From the time I was an adolescent, I dreamed of enjoying my glory years—a magical span of time I figured would fall somewhere between acne and wrinkles, when I would look and feel my best at all times. Emphasis on *looking* my best.

I recalled my glory years theory not too long ago and came to the alarming realization that if I had any at all, I likely missed them. I guess I was too busy enforcing nap times or wiping wet noses to notice just how stunning I looked.

It is just as well, I told myself. It is all vanity anyway.

Really?

Pretty Pretty, Likey Likey

We women pay special attention to beauty. My dad always notes with amusement that women don't fuss over their hair, makeup, and shoes to impress the men in their lives. More often than not, we dress to impress other women. After all, who is more likely to notice your striking new hair color or perfect pair of heels, your husband or a female friend?

We paint our fingernails. We decorate our homes. We enjoy enhancing and adorning our surroundings as well as our own bodies. Even after decades of popular culture's rejection of traditional stereotypes, flowers and jewelry remain perennially popular gifts for women. Because we like them. Because they are pretty.

God gave us hearts and eyes for beautiful things, but he made *us* beautiful as well. It is no accident that many of the world's most universally renowned works of art feature women as their subjects. Feminine beauty symbolizes the apex of creation. Mona Lisa, Venus de Milo, and you—*yes, you!*—are manifestations of God's abundant, creative beauty.

St. John Paul II noted the power and importance of women's beauty and found in it a reflection of our universal call to motherhood.

> The whole exterior of woman's body, its particular look, the qualities that stand, with the power of perennial attraction, at the beginning of the "knowledge" about which Genesis 4:1-2 speaks ("Adam united himself with Eve"), *are in strict union with motherhood.* With the simplicity characteristic of it, the Bible (and the liturgy following it) honors and praises throughout the centuries "the womb that bore you and the breasts from which you sucked milk" (Luke 11:27). These words are a eulogy of motherhood, of femininity, of the feminine body in its typical expression of creative love.[2]

Beauty is not a bad thing—it is a good thing! It is a natural virtue to which people are drawn. God made us in his image, and so the physical beauty of the human body is an attractive force that offers a glimmer of God himself—a hint, if you will, at the beatific vision itself. True beauty is not the "idol" our culture makes it, but an "icon" that points us toward heaven and gives us a glimpse of God.

More Important Than Things

The media, however, sometimes fails to connect a woman's physical beauty to the dignity of her motherly vocation. Have you

---

[2]   John Paul II. *Man and Woman He Created Them: A Theology of the Body,* trans. Michael Waldstein (Boston: Pauline Books & Media, 2006), no. 21, 5.

seen a *Glamour* magazine cover recently? *Sexy Hair! Flatter Abs in Days! Get the Butt You Want! Naughty Tricks that Pleasure Your Man!* Cover lines like these do not exactly respect the dignity of a woman as a complete person, body and soul.

Even as individuals, we sometimes separate human bodies from souls. We see and value only physical beauty. In our minds, we reduce others, especially women, and sometimes even ourselves, to mere bodies, sexual objects to be used for pleasure. This, John Paul II notes, is a weakness brought about by original sin. "The beauty that the human body possesses in its male and female appearance, as an expression of the spirit, is obscured."[3]

Because of sin, we see the world, ourselves, and each other through twisted lenses. We must remind ourselves that true human beauty encompasses both body and soul. Valuing human bodies over souls or human souls over bodies is a sin that denies our human dignity. We are not just a body. We are not just a soul. Our humanity is comprised of both, and both are integral to our dignity and worth.

It can be hard for a mom to see that sometimes. It is out of necessity that most moms abandon their dreams of glamour and sophistication. Like nothing else, the busyness of motherhood has the ability to sap the "pretty" right out of a girl. I know this as well as anyone.

One day, a few months after our sixth child was born, I piled the kids into the van for an afternoon of errands. I went to three different stores, chatted with clerks and customers, and even ran into a couple of acquaintances before returning home to discover

---

[3] John Paul II, *Man and Woman He Created Them: A Theology of the Body*, trans. Michael Waldstein (Boston: Pauline Books & Media, 2006), No. 32, 6.

that I had white dribbles of dried baby spit-up in my hair and a telltale trickle down the back of my shirt. Not so "glam."

Most of us know that God does not want us to be excessively concerned with our physical appearance. Nonetheless, because he has given us an eye for physical beauty—and because we live in a culture saturated with objectified images of feminine beauty—the desire to maintain youthful attractiveness can remain a tricky and emotional issue.

I am blessed to count as friends and sisters many lovely, talented, and inspiring women. Nearly every woman I have ever known personally, however, has at some point expressed dissatisfaction with her physical appearance. Few of us are immune to the temptation to look in the mirror and obsess about flabby thighs, uneven skin tone, or gray hairs. Others fight painful inner battles against frustration and even bitterness as they contemplate all the ways their womanly parts have prevented them from living out the motherly vocation as they had longed to do. Perhaps you can relate to this, too.

Even so, rest assured: Women are created to enjoy beauty and to be beautiful—a fact that is both a privilege and a responsibility.

Material Girls

Most of us struggle with unrealistic standards of beauty. It is nearly impossible to avoid comparing ourselves with physical perfection when images of the physically impossible bombard us daily.

A particularly compelling video I once saw on YouTube was a time-lapsed short film of a model getting ready for a photo shoot.[4] At the start of the video, the model is an attractive, but rather ordinary-looking young woman. After hours of professional makeup and hairstyling, however, she is unrecognizable as the same person. Even after the shoot, her photo—her very body—is re-touched and enhanced on a computer screen before finally being published on a billboard for hapless everyday women walking by to compare themselves with.

"You see?" I told my daughters as we watched the video together. "Not even the models really look like that."

It is an important lesson for all of us to remember. Impossible standards of physical perfection have never been more prevalent and dangerous to our feminine souls than they are today. Our media-saturated culture leaves little opportunity for real mothers with real bodies that have birthed real babies to feel good about themselves. The temptation is either to obsess and despair about all the ways we fall short of physical perfection or to pull on a ratty pair of yoga pants and give up altogether.

But God wants better than that for us.

You might never see real maternal curves on the cover of *Vogue*, but they are part of a woman's natural beauty and glory as God intends it. John Paul II recognized that, but do you? Do you know it in your heart?

Do you know that every part of your motherhood, all the way down to the physical changes it causes in your body, are part

---

[4]   http://www.youtube.com/watch?v=TOBMbHbXVOg.

of God's particular plan for you as a woman, wife, mother, and daughter of a King?

Wait! Don't slam the book closed! I promise not to wax poetic about stretch-marked bellies and saggy breasts!

The same applies to women who on a very basic level feel that their bodies have betrayed them through infertility or miscarriage, on one hand, or who feel overwhelmed with the physical toll of motherhood on the other. It can be hard to remember sometimes that inner beauty is reflected in our physical form. Think of Blessed Teresa of Calcutta, whose inner beauty and love never failed to shine through her wrinkled face and shrunken body. Here was a woman who positively radiated feminine beauty and joy.

We need to recognize that the gap that exists between plastic media images of beauty and the reality of what we see in the mirror is not our fault. It is the fault of a culture that devalues the vocation of motherhood, both its physical expressions and its hidden, self-donating charisms. *Instead of beating ourselves up for falling short of photoshopped perfection, we need to put our flaws into perspective.* To the extent that we embrace authentic femininity and motherhood, we will come to recognize the physical changes of motherhood not as flaws and failures, but as identifying marks of our God-given calling as women.

Beautiful Moms

I am sorry, ladies, but we need to talk about the ratty yoga pants.

Motherhood is not an excuse to neglect our appearance. There is no virtue in dowdiness. In fact, because we are teaching the next generation of Catholic women to understand their full dignity and worth, it is up to us to take good care of ourselves. If our real feminine beauty is a gift God means for us to give to the world, and in a special way to our husbands, we have a responsibility to care for our physical bodies.

Taking care of yourself does not have to mean getting up at the crack of dawn every day for marathon training, but it might mean following a reasonable diet and adding exercise to your daily routine in order to shed some extra pounds.

Paying attention to your appearance does not have to mean spending your children's college funds on hair extensions, stiletto heels, and haute couture, but it might mean getting an up-to-date haircut and investing a bit of time and effort in obtaining a few basic pieces of flattering clothing.

God made you a woman. He made you a living, breathing testimony to the glory and beauty of his creation. If we recognize and respect that fact, we will see that spending some amount of time and energy on our physical appearance is not vanity. It is a sacred duty—a reflection of the fact that we, too, have been made in the divine image of our Creator.

Be the Mom You Are

I have often found that the perfect antidote to compulsive self-criticism lies in embracing the motherly role I so often blame for having missed my "glory years" in the first place. God made us to be mothers and God made us to be beautiful. We need to remember that these two go hand in hand.

One recent Sunday morning, by a freak alignment of the stars or something, I actually managed to spend ten uninterrupted minutes in the bathroom getting ready before Mass. I dressed, brushed my hair, concealed dark circles, and even put on some lipstick. *Lipstick!* I kid you not. This was a big deal.

When I emerged from the bathroom, my young daughter Juliette, an aspiring princess in her own right, looked me over and gushed, "Oh, Mama! You are just *too pretty!*"

As I knelt to hug her, I looked over her shoulder and caught a glimpse of my husband beaming in our direction.

Noted. These are my glory years, and I am every bit as gorgeous as I need to be.

Such Beautiful Stuff

Most moms I know do not readily recognize themselves as subject to the temptation of materialism.

"Are you kidding me?" a friend laughed once when I brought up the subject. "I don't have time to be a fashion plate. I'm just glad if I get my shirt on right-side-out in the morning."

She had a point—and was wearing a pair of "mom jeans" to prove it.

But even those of us hanging out in mom jeans have to admit that the temptations of materialism are not limited to handbags and clothing. Let's talk about remodeling the bathroom, upgrading your dishwasher, and acquiring a shiny new minivan with a built-in DVD player. Let's talk about the items on your Amazon wish list, those perfectly adorable baby dresses you picked up on a whim last week, or the new cell phone that is smarter than you are.

Hmmm, did I just see your eyes light up anywhere in that list, "Mrs. Non-Material Mom"?

"I am always one major household appliance away from perfect happiness," a mom I know once joked. Or maybe she was not joking.

I will never forget the summer when my washer, dryer, and dishwasher all died dramatic and painful deaths in the same week. We had some other debts to pay off before we could afford to buy replacements, so I ... suffered.

Oh, how I suffered! And complained about my "suffering."

For weeks, I schlepped the family laundry to the laundromat, hung it outdoors to dry, and washed all of our dishes by hand. For weeks, I convinced myself that true human happiness lay in an unlimited credit line at Lowe's.

"I just want to be normal!" I whined shamelessly to my patient and frustratingly frugal husband after one particularly long, appliance-deprived day. He only smiled, but my bratty words were significant. We all want to be "normal," don't we? But how do we determine what "normal" means?

Most Americans would not call themselves rich by any means and yet, by the standards of the rest of the world, pretty much every one of us qualifies as wealthy. A family of four earning $50,000 per year, for example, is richer than ninety percent of the world's population. Even a family of four that earns just $22,000 per year—

considered poverty level in the United States—is still richer than eighty percent of the world's population.[5]

I am not at all saying that it is wrong to enjoy material goods, pleasures, and conveniences. The week at the end of that memorable summer when all of my new appliances were purchased, delivered, and installed was a glorious one indeed. I am saying that we need to carefully examine our attachment to material possessions and the power we give them to control our personal happiness.

Our natural feminine appreciation for beauty can trap us when we let it lead us into materialism. When we put our trust in material things—whether Prada handbags or Bosch dishwashers—we are sure to be disappointed.

It is only when we place our trust in God and discern our self-worth through a real and dynamic relationship with him that we will find happiness. The particular kind of happiness God has planned for you in this world may or may not include a front-load washer. For your sake, I sure hope it does, though. Like any woman, I am rather attached to my new laundry machines. And by "rather attached," I mean DON'T YOU DARE TAKE THESE THINGS AWAY FROM ME.

I might still have some detachment work to do. How about you? Let's finish up with a quick quiz to find out.

---

[5] GivingWhatWeCan.org.

Are You a Material Girl?

Answer TRUE or FALSE to the following:

_____ 1. When I look in the mirror, I am usually pleased
with what I see.

_____ 2. It would be nice to win the lottery, but God really
does provide adequately for our needs.

_____ 3. I know that my body is a beautiful gift from God,
imperfections and all.

_____ 4. I spend at least a little time every day taking care
of myself physically (exercise, hair, clothing, and
makeup).

_____ 5. When someone tells me I look nice, I accept the
compliment graciously.

If you answered FALSE to #1, you may need to work on accepting your physical flaws. Make a list of your best physical attributes. If you think you cannot do this, ask your husband or a trusted friend to help. Then, find a way to accentuate those attractive details of your appearance. Could your shiny hair use a new cut and style? Could you bring out the green of your eyes with a bit of eyeliner and mascara? Do something small, and do it every day. And then give thanks to God for his gift of beauty and the opportunity to give him glory through it.

If you answered FALSE to #2, you may need more practice in trusting God. Read and reflect on Matthew 6:25-26:

> Therefore I tell you, do not be anxious about your life, what you shall eat or what you shall drink, nor about your body, what you shall put on. Is not life more than food, and the body more than clothing? Look at the birds of the air: they neither sow nor reap nor gather into barns, and yet your heavenly Father feeds them. Are you not of more value than they?

Commit these verses to memory and recite them when financial or material concerns threaten your peace of mind. (3:00 AM? You know who you are.)

If you answered FALSE to #3, you probably need some help accepting the bodily changes that come with motherhood. Think of the many ways your body is a gift to yourself, your husband, and your family.

If you have biological children, recall the times when they gestated within your womb, growing and developing in the naturally nurturing environment of your own flesh and blood. What a

perfect gift to be that perfect means of sustenance to a tiny soul
you love.

Even those women who are not mothers experience giving
physical comfort: We comfort others with our arms. Soothe them
with our voice. Love them, serve them, and guide them with our
hands. Give thanks to God for the privilege of being the perfect
bodily gift to meet the needs of those you love and cherish.

If you answered FALSE to #4, the remedy is simple: Just do it.
No excuses. Even if you think your husband does not care (and I
do not know a man who does not care, at least a tiny bit, about his
wife's personal appearance), even if you think it is a silly waste of
time, take seriously your feminine call to beauty.

We do not all look like runway models. (Thank goodness! Have
you seen those poor, starved little girls? Makes me want to sneak
them a bag of donuts.) God made you beautiful, not just on the
inside, but on the outside, too. Taking proper care of the gift of
your physical body and enhancing your personal appearance is
both a privilege and a sacred duty.

If you answered FALSE to #5, spend some time in prayer:

Dear God,

Help me to see myself through your loving eyes. Turn off the voices of criticism that run through my head and replace them with words of thanksgiving for the beauty you have created in me. I want to give you glory in all things, from the words I speak to the physical beauty I share with the world. Let the light of your grace shine through me and fall upon all those I meet today.

Amen.

Make this promise to yourself right now: The next time someone compliments my appearance, I will smile brightly. I will say, "thank you," and nothing else.

Chapter 3

Nothing More Than Feelings

"But Mary kept all these things, pondering them in her heart."

—Luke 2:19

Strength:
We feel things deeply.

Weakness:
We let our emotions rule
and wind up unbalanced
and unhappy.

My husband has not studied the five love languages. He rarely uses "I feel" statements. And until they start holding them in a boat on a lake during peak bass season, he is unlikely to attend any kind of "marriage encounter" weekend. Even so, he is a master communicator.

Case in point: Just the other evening, when our two-year-old son was clinging to my leg and whining in the kind of piercing pitch that only two-year-old vocal chords can produce, Dan said to me, "My dear and darling wife, you do so much for the family and me. You made a delicious dinner and cleaned up the kitchen all by yourself. Why don't you take a well-deserved break in the other room while I handle this unruly toddler for a while?"

What's that? You don't believe he said those things?

Well, he did. He just didn't use words. He used a quick look of sympathy and a slight smile of amusement at his young son's obnoxious behavior before scooping him onto his lap with a nod in my direction. And I got it.

Such is the language of long-married couples. It consists not of words, but of grunts, sighs, glances, smiles, squints, and an occasional well-arched eyebrow. We speak our own private, wordless language, and we understand one another because, more often than not, we truly are one.

I loved the familiar "two shall become one" passage from Genesis that was read at our wedding, but for me back then those words only inspired romantic notions of marital unity. I was naive and inexperienced. I thought that "two shall become one" meant long nights spent gazing into one another's eyes and talking about our feelings.

Well, eighteen years and eight kids later, Dan and I surely have had some long nights. But they have mostly consisted of colicky babies, Tylenol doses, and passing the vomit bucket, rather than any kind of "feelings talk."

Ah, feelings. We ladies do love our feelings, don't we?

We love them so much, we might just drive everyone around us crazy with our obsession about sharing them, discussing them, making sure others are sensitive to them, and enticing our loved ones to explore theirs as well.

I remember one Sunday morning during the early years of our marriage. Dan and I were racing through the house before Mass in typical fashion. There were last-minute diaper changes, lost socks, crabby toddlers, and ... my sore feelings from an argument that took place the night before.

I do not remember what the argument was about, but I do remember that I decided that right there in the midst of our "Sunday scramble" was a perfectly reasonable time to accuse my husband of not caring about me and my feelings.

"What are you talking about?" Dan shot back in exasperation. "Look at me!"

I looked at him. He was crouched on the floor, a diaper bag slung over one shoulder, coaxing a small buckle shoe onto our squirming daughter's reluctant foot. How was that for feelings? Would a man who did not care *choose* to spend his Sunday morning like this?

I needed to decide. Did I want a man who shared his feelings and was focused on my emotions? Or did I want a man who shared my circumstances and was focused on heavenly goals for ourselves and our children? A man who was unafraid of self-sacrifice, of getting down on the floor—and getting dirty in the process?

I don't know about you, but I chose the latter. And good thing, too, because that's what I've got.

Inevitably, if you stick around long enough, romantic love becomes a different kind of love—one that is more about charitable unity than romantic intensity. Couples speak the same language. They have the same goals. They are on the same team. But hopelessly romantic and feelings-based or not, it is still love.

It has been said that relationships often go through three basic stages—romance, disillusionment, and joy. Many of us are familiar with the fact that in a long-term relationship, romance comes to an end. This does not mean you no longer love each other or do romantic things together, but the courting phase of your relationship changes to a much more practical one, where the everyday grind becomes more the norm than candlelit dinners and love notes. If a couple can make it through the challenging, post-romance phase of marriage, the relationship often evolves into a deep, abiding joy. One reason is that you both have "fought the good fight" together—you have raised your family to adulthood (and all the challenges that come with it)—and you each realize that it was your spouse who did it with you.

Shared Feelings vs. Shared Goals

That question I asked myself that Sunday morning years ago was the key to a kind of "growing up" I needed to do in my marriage, as a woman and as a wife. We might think we want a man who is focused on our feelings, but emotions often can blur our vision and blind us to the value of the real relationships we have.

Don't get me wrong. Feelings *are* important. And as women, we have the all-important job, it sometimes seems, of doing the better part of "feeling" for the entire world.

I once worked with a young woman who was a bit of a hippie. She was agnostic, too, so at first glance, I would not have thought the two of us would have much in common. I was pleasantly surprised, though, to find that we shared a common appreciation for the unique value of women and God's plan (whether she wanted to call it that or not) for the gift of feminine genius.

The two of us often talked about how women are the caregivers and nurturers of our world, how we are life-givers and relationship-builders. I will never forget the day my co-worker waxed poetic about female menstruation, of all things.

"I really believe," she told me dreamily, "that women bleed for the whole world. The whole world is in pain, and we are the ones who feel it."

I told you she was earthy. But she was on to something there—something authentically Catholic. Our monthly cycles are a sign of our uniquely feminine capacity to conceive and nurture new life. Our fertility and all of its outward signs are indeed a gift, to our families as well as the world at large. We are also unique in our capacity to feel, to empathize, and to offer love and compassion to our fellow human beings. These are gifts we are meant to use to bless our families, our communities, and our world.

We Sob Because We Care

When it was time for cake and ice cream following my eight-year-old son's birthday dinner a couple of years ago, I donned a pair of sunglasses. My husband and kids knew exactly why I went for the eye cover. It was to spare my dignity.

You see, our family has a birthday tradition of taking turns around the table, sharing things we especially love and appreciate about the person celebrating a birthday. Without fail, every time we do this, and I listen to my children compliment, encourage, and appreciate one another, I turn into a sobbing puddle of mush.

I am a crier. I will not try to deny it. I am not so much of a crier about personally disappointing or sad things, mind you. I think even my husband would admit that I am not the kind of woman who quickly turns to tears in a crisis or during an argument. I am at least a little bit tough that way. But I sure do make up for my tough side when it comes to sentimental things. Like movies, for example.

It's a Wonderful Life? Heaps of sobbing.

The Notebook? Mascara mayhem.

Marley and Me? My tear ducts might never recover.

My family has grown accustomed to the fact that at birthday parties, New Year's celebrations, and in the face of any especially sweet gesture of love or kindness, I dissolve into tears instantly.

"Mama's crying again!" Some snicker and some sigh. But don't they know? I only sob because I care.

St. John Paul II recognized the unique value of women's capacity to feel deeply in today's world. In *Mulieris Dignitatem*, he writes:

> In our own time, the successes of science and technology make it possible to attain material well-being to a degree hitherto unknown. While this favors some, it pushes others to the edges of society. In this way, unilateral progress can also lead to a gradual *loss of sensitivity for man, that is, for what is essentially human.* In this sense, our time in particular *awaits the manifestation* of that "genius" which belongs to women, and which can ensure sensitivity for human beings in every circumstance: because they are human!—and because 'the greatest of these is love' (cf. 1 Corinthians 13:13).[1]

His profound insights into the important calling of wives and mothers, celebrating the "feminine genius," made St. John Paul II one of the most beloved popes of all time. He understood intuitively that we women are our family's folders and sorters, but we are also our family's *feel*-ers. Maybe we notice more than we should. We might pay attention to all the tiny details. We might blubber at birthdays, remember every blessed thing, and love so much it embarrasses the kids.

I will not apologize for that. Our jaded world could use a little extra heartfelt love and emotion. Tears are a tangible sign of the intensity of our affection. Doesn't every family, every human being, deserve that kind of "to-the-moon-and-back" devotion?

---

[1] *Mulieris Dignitatem* 30.

Emotional Overboard

Feminine feelings are a physical reality. Do you ever wonder why you feel so much better after a good cry? It's chemical.

The chemical makeup of emotional tears is quite different from the normal moisture in your eyes or the kind of fluid your eyes produce as a result of injury or irritation. Emotional crying produces chemical tears—loaded with proteins, manganese, and the hormone prolactin, which builds up in the body in response to stress or arousal.

But we already know all about hormones, don't we? Many of us suffer from mood swings, anxiety, irritability, and mild depression that fluctuate with our monthly cycles. These emotional challenges can be exacerbated by pregnancy, breastfeeding, and menopause.

Though I like to think I am pretty levelheaded and even-tempered most of the time, I must admit that I have succumbed to the powers of the hormones many times in my life, especially during pregnancy. I can remember the feeling of helplessness I had when, while pregnant with our fifth child, I found myself furiously angry with my husband over some minor disagreement. And when I say "furiously angry," I mean so mad I heard pounding in my ears and could not see straight.

In that moment, I had enough presence of mind to recognize that my feelings were far more dramatic than the situation called for and that my anger was not fair to Dan. And yet I could not help it. I just was that angry.

I would like to say that I handled the situation with grace, but I am not so sure I did. I am pretty sure there were some heartfelt apologies and that some cathartic tears were shed afterward. But the fact that I recognized the irrationality and imbalance of my emotions in that moment was a revelation for me. I realized that while I might not always be able to control how I feel, I can indeed work to control the ways in which I express those feelings.

To do that, I realized I needed to develop the life skills required to (1) recognize when my feelings were over the top and (2) find a safe and fair way to calm myself down before using my feelings as a weapon to bludgeon those I profess to love.

Let's talk about some of those life skills.

The first step that anyone should take if she suspects that she needs a hormonal intervention, is to make an appointment with a trusted professional. Clinical depression and anxiety are serious matters that should be diagnosed and treated, but even much lesser kinds of imbalances can be controlled or improved with hormone therapy or other measures.

Your Ob-Gyn or midwife could be a good place to start, or you might consider contacting a fertility care professional that specializes in NaProtechnology, a new women's health science that monitors and maintains female reproductive and gynecological health. NaProtechnology includes medical and surgical treatments that cooperate completely with a woman's natural cycles and reproductive system.[2]

---

[2]   Find a practitioner at *naprotechnology.com*.

Communication Is Key

The first life skill every woman should work on—especially when feeling hormonal—is communication. Choose a moment when your thinking is unclouded by any kind of hormonal haze and talk with your husband, your children, and anyone else who is a potential victim of your emotions. Tell them how much you love them and admit that you sometimes struggle with controlling your emotions, which are not always balanced and appropriate. Tell them you are working on this, and ask them to pray for you.

I have found that having these kinds of frank conversations is very helpful to my children especially, because though I want to model responsible and appropriate behavior for them, I sometimes fall short of that mark. We all fall short sometimes, and getting our families on board with our plan to improve is an important step toward healing.

In the Moment

Frank communication beforehand is also helpful when you anticipate a difficult moment ahead of you and you are concerned about becoming angry or overly sad about some trifling matter. If your husband already understands that you sometimes have these kinds of challenges, he will be more inclined to support you when you tell him, "I need some time to calm down before I talk to you about that," or some similar sentiment.

And then, take that time to calm down. Eat a brownie. Call a girlfriend. Take a hot shower and maybe sob a bit. Even St. Thomas

Aquinas, a great doctor of the Church, advised that sorrow can often be alleviated by good sleep, a bath, and a glass of wine.[3]

He left out the chocolate and the crying, but he was a man, after all.

Prevent Problems

Finally, I cannot end this chapter without mentioning some of the simple ways we can keep ourselves balanced, both physically and emotionally. I will warn you—they are boring. And you have likely heard them before. But today I want you to hear them with new ears—with a heart and mind that newly recognize the unique gift you have to offer the world with your capacity to feel and the unique responsibility you have to nurture and use that gift in balanced ways in service to others.

You Need Sleep

How much do you sleep each night? While some maternal sleep deprivation is inevitable, we can all make getting proper rest a bigger priority, especially during times when we feel stressed and unbalanced. There are days when you will need to skip the chores and other work you usually tackle during your child's naptime, and take a nap with your toddler. If you work outside the home, take fifteen minutes in the middle of the day to find a quiet place to close your eyes and breathe deeply, offering back to God all the little details of your day that keep you feeling off-balance and distracted. At the end of particularly exhausting days, go home, turn off the television, close the laptop, and go to bed early. Keep a pen and paper on your nightstand so you can write down the "to do's" and other ideas that leave you staring at the ceiling. Avoid

---

[3]   See *Summa Theologica* I-IIae, q. 38, art. 5

caffeine and other stimulants that might interfere with regular sleep. Consider these small efforts a gift you give to yourself ... and to your family.

You Need Exercise

I know you know this. That is why you are rolling your eyes right now. Well, I am here to say: Stop that! If you struggle with anger, anxiety, or any form of depression and you are not exercising regularly, you are refusing to provide basic care for your body, which is not healthy. Scientific studies have shown that regular exercise releases endorphins, the body's "feel good" hormones, which can be as effective as a mild antidepressant. No excuses: Walk, run, dance, stretch, swim, bike, skate, jump, or spin. I do not care what you do, but move your body. Take care of *you*.

Besides physical exercise, we often need to give ourselves a spiritual workout as well. We are all familiar with the idea of our muscles becoming flabby from underuse, but did you know that the same is true of your spiritual muscles? If you are not regularly practicing the virtues that offset your particular vices, you are in danger of growing spiritually weak and vulnerable.

A couple of years ago, I took up running regularly as my primary source of physical exercise, and for the most part, I have really enjoyed making running a part of my daily routine. On a neighborhood running route I take regularly that includes a small hill, though, I noticed something. As a beginning runner, when I ran uphill, my immediate mental response was to give up. The incline would challenge my legs and lungs to work harder, and my involuntary mental response was to quit. Right away.

Must stop now, my mind would scream, just a few paces into the hill.

I was unpleasantly surprised by my wimpy reaction, and I decided that I did not want to be the kind of person who gives up at the first sign of a challenge, whether physical or mental. I was determined to "fix" this part of myself, and I realized that the remedy for feeling weak in the face of running uphill was to run up many hills. Big hills, faster and harder, a few days a week, until I had taught my mind and body not to shut down in the face of an uphill challenge. It worked beautifully. I no longer fall apart when facing a hill while running.

The same is true of spiritual exercises. The remedy for any spiritual weakness you might find in yourself is to face it and conquer it, again and again, seeking appropriate help if you need it. If you struggle with patience, for example, you might "exercise" patience by doing a jigsaw puzzle with a preschooler a few times a week, focusing on making it a patient and loving interaction. If you lack trust or faith, you might "exercise" by challenging yourself to let go of areas of anxiety in your life, or by inserting time for Adoration in your weekly schedule. If you struggle with pride, you can exercise spiritually by giving yourself the assignment of complimenting at least three other people each day or performing a particularly humble task in service to others on a regular basis.

You get the idea. Find out what your spiritual "hills" are, and then assign yourself some to run up, every day, until you conquer those hills. Then move on to the next uphill challenge.

You Need Good Food

You know this, too, but just in case you missed the memo: What you eat matters. It affects how you look, feel, and function every day. Even if an unbalanced diet is not making you fat (some of the unhealthiest eaters I know are naturally very thin people), it is affecting how you feel. Do you feel sluggish or irritable? Sugar or processed foods might be contributing to your problem. Give your body a fighting chance at achieving balance by taking small steps toward eating better. Add some whole grains; skip some sugar. Add some green leafy vegetables; skip some fast food. Add some water; skip some caffeinated soda. You know what to do. You just need to recognize the importance of it and make it a bigger priority.

Besides physical nourishment, we women need spiritual nourishment as well. Just as our physical cravings cue us into physical imbalances in our bodies, spiritual longings are an indication of the state of our hearts and souls.

What kind of "soul food" do you crave? Does God feel far away, and do you long for a more personal connection with Jesus? A date with him in Eucharistic Adoration might be a good idea for your next "meal." If you find yourself feeling disillusioned and unloved by God, spending some time performing acts of charity might be a good remedy for your isolation, or perhaps some time spent reading the writings of the saints, like Blessed Teresa of Calcutta, who shared your feelings. If you feel spiritually unbalanced and distracted, you might consider scheduling a small amount of time, perhaps first thing in the morning, for personal prayer, reading, or reflection.

I think sometimes we put off prayer, especially during busy times, because it feels too much like work. It feels like one more thing to "do," and we are exhausted already from so much doing. I know I still fall prey to this way of thinking now and then. *I do not have time to pray today,* I sometimes think late in the day. *Once I get the kids in bed and the kitchen cleaned up, there will not be a minute left.*

I need to remind myself often that prayer is not a chore; it is not a "to-do" that demands a certain number of minutes from my schedule each day. Prayer is a relationship and a communion with God. My Creator. The Being for whom I was created. The One for whom I long and without whom I am restless and lost. Prayer is engaging in a soul-feeding relationship that strengthens and renews me.

Now, that all sounds very nice, you might be thinking, *but praying a Rosary (and certainly gathering the family for one) absolutely does take time. It takes time to read the psalms in the morning, and it takes time to go to daily Mass. Heck, it takes time to say my Morning Offering first thing in the morning while the kids pound on the locked bathroom door.*

And, of course, you are right. This kind of formal prayer does take time, and it is worthy soul food when you can make space in your day for it. But it is not the only kind of prayer that can feed our souls. We can nurture our relationship with God, all day, every day, simply by turning our hearts toward him. During quieter moments in our days, even if our hands are busy folding laundry, changing diapers, and doing dishes, we can turn our mind toward God and maintain an interior silence as we dwell in his presence.

If you make an effort to "pray" in these small ways and develop a habit of making your relationship with God the center of your life, even as you are busy doing dozens of other things, your soul will find peace. You will find yourself seeking to make more time for God in your life, even in ways that take more of your time. We are not built to be alone. We are not independent creatures; we are entirely dependent upon God. We find lasting peace and contentment only by pursuing a real relationship with him through prayer.

Now that we have explored some of the ways our feminine sensitivities and emotions can be both a blessing and a burden, let's find out how much you struggle with balancing your emotions and discover some ways you can work toward achieving greater balance.

Are You an
Emotional Roller Coaster?

Answer TRUE or FALSE to the following:

_____ 1. PMS gives me license to lose my temper, and my family should just understand.

_____ 2. I am sometimes embarrassed by my emotionalism—crying about silly things or suddenly becoming very angry.

_____ 3. I can name three healthy ways to vent stressful feelings.

_____ 4. I know that my sensitivity is a gift from God, and I do my best to use it in service to others.

_____ 5. When my emotions are difficult to manage, I bring them to God.

If you answered TRUE to #1, we need to talk. More specifically, *you* need to talk—to your doctor, to your family, to a trusted friend, to a priest. While it absolutely is true that the hormones associated with pregnancy, breastfeeding, menopause, and monthly cycles are more challenging for some women than for others, having this kind of challenge in your life is not a free pass to be obnoxious or, worse yet, to hurt those you love. We all struggle to find balance in some areas of our lives; we all suffer some kinds of weaknesses that, while they make "being good" more difficult, do not absolve us of the responsibility to treat others fairly. If you suspect that you might be indulging your emotional weaknesses at the expense of your family, get some support and make the first step toward improvement by admitting that it is not OK and letting your family know that you are working on it.

If you answered TRUE to #2, repeat after me: "God made me a woman, and a woman is a very good thing to be." An important part of being a healthy, joyful woman is accepting the ways in which you are different from a man. You cannot control what you feel, but you can control how you manage and express your feelings. You might feel a bit awkward when you tear up while talking to the dentist about your son's flossing habits, but fear not. We all do the crazy crying thing now and then. It is important business. We feel for the world, and the world would be a dark and empty place without our feelings. Put on a pair of sunglasses and rock on, Mom!

If you answered FALSE to #3, let's brainstorm right now about some healthy ways you can vent negative emotions, anger, and stress. We talked about a few at the end of the chapter (resting properly, exercising regularly, and eating well), but there are hundreds of other ways you can get the emotional release you need. Laughter is a big one. Do you maintain a sense of humor about your life and about your emotional challenges in particular? Connecting with friends is another important one. And what about those times when you find yourself needing what I like to call a "sanity moment"?

Write down a few things you can do at a moment's notice when you need a lift: Ride a bike, knead some dough, do your nails, paint a picture, watch a funny movie, write a letter, call your mom, sing out loud, tell a story, look at old pictures, bake some banana bread, brew some tea, play with modeling clay, eat something delicious, listen to music, write in your journal, curl your hair, do thirty squats, go outside, scrub the bathtub, take a nap ... you can probably think of dozens more.

The key is to have a plan for positively dealing with negative emotions—whether it is stress, anger, sadness, or anxiety—so that you do not let one poor decision spiral downward into many more before you come out of your funk.

If you answered FALSE to #4, begin to cultivate a habit of thinking and speaking about your emotions in a positive way. Think of a woman in your life who has blessed you with her compassion and understanding—perhaps a mother, a sister, or a close friend. Think of our Blessed Mother at the wedding at Cana, noticing that the hosts were out of wine and bringing this to the attention of her son. What small needs of others can you notice and help serve today? Thank Mother Mary for her example and ask her to open your eyes to the ways God is calling you to do the same in your life.

If you answered FALSE to #5, here is a prayer that might help. Go ahead and tear it out of the book and tape it to your bathroom mirror, for those moments when you really need it. And in the meantime, why not offer it to God right now?

A Mother's Prayer for Peace

I know that you made me a woman and that every part of my femininity is meant to be a gift to the world and to my family in particular. Help me to see my emotions for the gift that they are. Inspire in me a desire to use my sensitivity in the service of others. Replace my selfishness with generosity; replace my anger with compassion; replace my anxiety with trust in you. Give me grace to pause in moments when I am tempted to misuse my gifts. Turn my heart to you, and give me strength to use all my talents and womanly gifts to bring you to others and to bring others to you. In the name of the Father, and of the Son, and of the Holy Spirit.

Amen.

Chapter 4

Perfect, Schmerfect

"And Mary said, 'My soul magnifies the Lord, and my spirit rejoices in God my Savior, for he has regarded the low estate of his handmaiden. For behold, henceforth all generations will call me blessed; for he who is mighty has done great things for me, and holy is his name.'"

—Luke 1:46-49

Strength:
We have high ideals.

Weakness:
We let "perfect" become the enemy of the "good" and become demanding and despairing.

Does this bumper sticker belong on your minivan? "I used to be a perfectionist, but I'm trying to improve."

No, really. Are you a perfectionist?

Some women I know announce their own "perfectionism" with what sounds like just a bit of pride. To be a "perfectionist," after all, one must be nearly perfect, nearly all the time. I would like to take a peek into their hall closets someday.

Other women I know talk about "perfectionism" with a wince and a sigh. These are the ones who have seen the ugly side of "perfect." Perhaps *you* experienced the dark side of perfection early on, when the perfectly uniform walls of your painstakingly crafted sugar-cube pyramid came crashing down right in front of the judges at the sixth-grade science fair. Or maybe it was that time you had a clever idea for a Halloween costume. After spending hours painting little squares on a cardboard box, you spent all of Halloween night explaining that no, you are not a brick wall. Any dunderhead could see that you were a *Rubik's Cube!*

Okay, so we might not all struggle beneath the crushing weight of "sugar-cube pyramid" perfection, but most of us know the ugly side of perfectionism. We all find ourselves falling short of our own high ideals and expectations at times.

Where do those high ideals and expectations come from, anyway? Much of it is self-induced and might be traced to a faulty understanding of certain Bible passages, such as:

> You, therefore, must be perfect, as your heavenly Father is perfect.
>
> —Matthew 5:48

That passage used to give me a stomachache. It is a rather tall order, isn't it? And yet, in many of us, there is an inclination toward a kind of pseudo-holy lifestyle, rooted in a well-intended (though undeniably self-centered) bid to win the attention and approval of both God and other Christians.

Of course, this is not what Jesus was talking about. To understand the real meaning of this passage, we need to look at the context of Christ's command. Before telling us to be "perfect," this is what he says:

> You have heard that it was said, "You shall love your neighbor and hate your enemy." But I say to you, love your enemies and pray for those who persecute you, so that you may be sons of your Father who is in heaven; for he makes his sun rise on the evil and on the good, and sends rain on the just and on the unjust. For if you love those who love you, what reward have you? Do not even the tax collectors do the same? And if you salute only your brethren, what more are you doing than others? Do not even the Gentiles do the same? (Matthew 5:43-47).

It still is a tall order, but the kind of perfection Christ demands of us is not made up of sparkling windowpanes, uncluttered countertops, organized spice racks, mopped floors, manicured fingernails, obedient children, or even well-vacuumed minivans. It is made up of love. Just like our heavenly Father is.

We need to admit that the perfection many of us seek—and then beat ourselves up for falling short of achieving—is most likely the earthly and human kind. More often than not, we are seeking not so much to reflect authentic love for the benefit of others, but to shine brightly for our own gratification.

There is nothing wrong with taking pride in a well-kept home, a job well done, or well-behaved children, but we are never meant to accomplish perfection in those things at the expense of heavenly perfection—which is love.

Perfection of Love

So what does that perfect kind of love look like? Sometimes it looks like letting go of our own ideals and expectations and embracing the reality of what God has placed in our path.

I once knew a phonics teacher, for example, who was adamantly opposed to "sight-reading," a method of reading that teaches words by sight recognition instead of "sounding out" and blending letter sounds. She was adamantly opposed to sight-reading, that is, until God gave her a beautifully "imperfect" daughter who was learning-disabled and could not learn to read any other way. It was then that she changed her idea of the "perfect" way to learn.

Bit by bit, life has a way of chipping away at the reality of what we think we know about the "perfect" or the "right" way of doing things. Like many women I know, I was a perfect parent ... before I had kids. Once those darn kids come along, the humbling process of learning to love them the way God has planned, instead of the "perfect" way we envision, begins.

It certainly did not take long for me. I was all of two weeks into this motherhood thing when I was forced to let go of some of my "perfect" plans.

My first child was a colicky baby. She started screaming the day after she was born, and for the next three months, she scarcely paused to breathe. Nearly two screeching weeks after Kateri's birth, my mother stopped by for an afternoon visit. I had probably placed a desperate phone call or two (or seventeen), and I am sure my mom, who raised nine children of her own, knew precisely what was going on in my tiny apartment.

"Why don't you go pick up some groceries and get some fresh air?" she gently nudged my bleary-eyed husband.

"Can I?" Dan stammered, looking at me for permission to leave.

Of course he could leave. And boy did he. In his dash toward the exit, he tripped over a partially assembled infant swing, brushed himself off, and without looking back shouted, "I'm fine!" as he lunged for the doorknob.

When he was gone, I placed my howling infant on the bed and my mother stood silently beside me. My mother has a wordless way about her that speaks volumes. Her very presence soothes and comforts, making me feel safe enough to express my innermost hurts and fears.

I burst into tears.

"This is all she ever does!" I shouted above the screaming.

Mom studied the two of us—sobbing daughter and screeching granddaughter. She bit her lower lip and wrinkled her brow.

"Maybe you should try a pacifier," she finally said.

I looked at her in disbelief. A pacifier? Was she serious? Did she not know that I had received about a dozen pacifiers as baby shower gifts and they were sitting, unopened, in a top dresser drawer because I had read volumes in preparation for this infant's arrival and was deathly afraid of "nipple confusion"?

You heard that right. Nipple confusion. Do not pretend you have never heard of it. And do not pretend you have never been afraid that your infant child would forget how to nurse and wither away to nothing because she grew accustomed to having a rubber pacifier nipple in her mouth instead of the real thing. OK, so maybe you have not. You will have to excuse my irrational, postpartum neuroses, but just know that the issue felt real to me at the time.

When my mother dared to say, "Maybe you should try a pacifier," I opened my mouth to educate her about the horrors of nipple confusion, but, much to my surprise, what came out instead was a gasping, grateful, "*Can I?*"

My mother looked on in amusement as I raced for the dresser drawer, grabbed the first package within reach, and popped a pacifier into my ecologically breastfed daughter's mouth.

Blessed silence blanketed the room. Kateri sucked silently and held the two of us in the same unnerving gaze I had seen minutes after her birth.

Was she confused already? She did not seem to be. She seemed only calm—at last calm and accepting of this place she had been born into, this mother she had been given, this life she was meant to live.

Of course, the moral of this story has nothing to do with the reality of "nipple confusion" or the advisability of giving babies pacifiers. These are often emotionally loaded parenting issues that are best left up to mothers and their babies to figure out, each for themselves.

The point is simply that this was the first of many parental moments in which I would finally let go of my own noisy plans and hear God's voice in the quiet: "Be still and know that I am God" (Psalm 46:10). *Be still.* I recalled the seeds of self-doubt planted during my pregnancy and again in the first moments I held my daughter in the hospital, after her birth, when I thought, *Can I do this?*

And it was only there, in the stillness, as I stood beside my mother, watching my infant daughter grow both calmer and potentially more nipple-confused by the moment, that I began to understand—just a little bit—that, *yes, I can!*

As my mother did before me, as my now eighteen-year-old daughter long ago understood, I can so do this. It is just that some parts of doing it are going to be different than the way I had planned.

Where Do We Find Our Worth?

This is all well and good, you might be thinking. It sounds very nice to say that we can make compromises and let go of our ideas of "perfection" in order to replace them with real love. But in a world where flashy headlines assure us of all the ways in which modern women can (and should) "do it all" and "have it all," it can be a crushing blow to our egos sometimes to admit that we cannot, and we do not. And we will not ever.

It stings to admit that we are weak and imperfect creatures, and it becomes all the more difficult when it seems that other women are indeed attaining the kind of domestic "perfection" we are drawn to. This is when we need to remind ourselves of the special calling, the dignity and worth, that all women have, especially as manifested by the unique responsibility God gives us through motherhood, both physical and spiritual.

We will not find our dignity, worth, and purpose in professional accomplishments, homemaking skills, parental perfection, or social status. We fulfill our greatest calling through the fact that God *entrusts* other human beings to our care. It is in acknowledging the respect the world owes to the importance of motherhood that we begin to recognize our momnipotence—the power and strength of every woman to change the world through her motherhood.

> The moral and spiritual strength of a woman is joined to her awareness that *God entrusts the human being to her in a special way.* Of course, God entrusts every human being to each and every other human being. But this entrusting concerns women in a special way—precisely by reason of their femininity—and this in a particular way determines their vocation. ...
>
> *A woman is strong because of her awareness of this entrusting,* strong because of the fact that God "entrusts the human being to her," always and in every way, even in the situations of social discrimination in which she may find herself. This awareness and this fundamental vocation speak to women of the dignity which they receive from God himself, and this makes them "strong" and strengthens their vocation.
>
> —St. John Paul II[1]

What John Paul II is saying here is that, in a special way, through physical and spiritual motherhood, God demonstrates a woman's dignity and worth. It is through motherhood that he gives us moral and spiritual strength. He places these tiny human beings, whom

---

[1]   *Mulieris Dignitatem* 30.

he loves with a greater love than we can comprehend, in *our* care. He gives them to us and trusts us to care for them, nurture them, and love them as only a mother can.

That is a big deal.

Mary knew this. She is the perfect example of the power and dignity that comes from this kind of entrusting. God chose Mary to bring Christ into the world. He chose her to care for him within her body, to nurse, feed, clothe, teach, and love him. It is through this special calling that she is blessed and gives glory to God. Let's read Mary's own words in the first chapter of Luke:

> And Mary said, "My soul magnifies the Lord, and my spirit rejoices in God my Savior, for he has regarded the low estate of his handmaiden. For behold, henceforth all generations will call me blessed; for he who is mighty has done great things for me, and holy is his name."
>
> —Luke 1:46-49

God does not do "great things" just for Mary. He does "great things" for every woman by offering her the dignity inherent in her vocation to motherhood. We find our own calling, our own happiness, and our own purpose for living when we give glory to God by answering his call to motherhood. Talk about momnipotent.

Special Calling, Special Distractions

The fact that we are called to love and serve others through the special vocation of motherhood inspires us to set high goals for ourselves and those we love. If God has found us worthy enough to entrust precious and vulnerable human beings to our care, we need to be up to the task. We are going to feed these children well, teach them well, discipline them well, and care for them in the very best ways possible.

Can you see where this is headed, though? Our high ideals and inspired motivation leave us vulnerable to distraction and despair. Our special calling makes us want the very best for those whom God entrusts to our care, but it is easy to get so focused on the details of the kind of care we are providing for our families that we lose sight of what really matters.

100 Percent Real Love

I paused in the supermarket aisle one recent weekday with an oversized cardboard box in my hand. I wanted to buy it—and yet something inside me recoiled at the thought of placing this particular item in my shopping cart.

My fingers clutched the cardboard as I studied the label: *100% Real Potatoes.* Mashed potatoes in minutes. Standing in the aisle of the grocery store at 4:30 PM with no real plan for dinner and a pint-sized Houdini intent on escaping the shopping cart harness, the idea was downright delicious.

And yet, I hesitated, because I used to be a cooking snob. Some small part of me still wants to claim that title. Once upon a time, everything from my kitchen was absolutely, positively made from scratch. Frozen waffles? Inferior! Bread from the store? Puh-leeze! Potatoes from a box? Unthinkable!

But I only had a few small children back then. Since that time, more babies have come along. I have had pregnancies where I wound up useless on the couch or kneeling in front of a toilet bowl for weeks on end. God has given me more bodies to feed, more clothing to launder, and more dishes to wash. Those first babies have grown older, and though I never run out of love, some days I surely have run out of time and energy.

Somewhere along the way, out of sheer necessity, I made some cooking concessions. With a family that could eat its way through a loaf of bread in a single lunchtime, I gave in to the convenience of the store-bought stuff. Homemade bread baking became a once-in-a-while treat. And ultimately, even a snob like me had to admit that brownies from a mix tasted lots better than no brownies at all.

I made these concessions, but not without some measure of guilt. Preparing exclusively homemade food for my family had been a point of pride for me. It had been a tangible way for me to assure myself I was a "good mom." I was fooling myself, but it was a comfortable con.

I have a friend who likes to tell her husband in the morning before he leaves for work: "I can do two out of these three things today: homeschool, keep the house clean, or make a good dinner. Which two would you like?"

I love this approach because I find it a helpful reminder that, no matter what *Cosmopolitan* magazine might try to sell us, none of us can "do it all." Besides, as every mother knows, even if we *did* find a way to do it all, it surely would not stay done. We must pick and choose the good things we will do. It is a continual balancing act.

Choosing Balance

And so we choose: I will serve lunch on paper plates, but I will read *Curious George Gets a Medal* later today. I will catch up on the laundry, but I will let that sticky spot on the kitchen tile sit for another day, or two, or ten. I will make muffins for an afternoon snack, but I will not answer emails. I will chat on the phone with a friend for thirty minutes, but I will not freak out if I forget to make my kids' dental appointments.

And sometimes I will buy the boxed potatoes—the alleged 100 percent real potatoes—for my 100 percent real life. I will stand at the stove with a toddler on my hip and stir instant potatoes with one hand while a whirlwind of family life encircles me. I will spell "immortal" for the nine-year-old who asks me. I will interrupt one grinning child's rendition of the "K-I-S-S-I-N-G" song with his brother's name in it before the affronted party resorts to death blows. And when my garrulous four-year-old asks, "Would you like to hear a story?" I will refrain from sighing and rolling my eyes. I will smile weakly and say, "Yes, sweetie. Talk to mama while I make dinner."

Today I will focus on the things I do right instead of the things I do wrong or that remain undone. I will find security and satisfaction in knowing that none of us can do it all, but that I am doing enough. None of us can have it all, but we can all have what really matters. I am not a perfect mom, but with God's grace I can be a great one. I can love as only a mother can love. I can give this family, right here, right now, 100 percent of the very best I have.

Do You Need a
Perfection Intervention?

Answer TRUE or FALSE to the following:

——— 1. When I meet a new female friend, one of the first things I notice are the ways in which she appears to be more perfect than I am.

——— 2. When it comes to housekeeping, there are certain tasks that only I can do, because only I can "do them right."

——— 3. I sometimes put off beginning important tasks indefinitely because I am waiting for "the time to be right" to do them.

——— 4. I know that God loves me unconditionally.

——— 5. When I fail at something, I readily turn to prayer to ask God, "What now?"

If you answered TRUE to #1, join the club. Every one of us has a tendency to do this sometimes. The trouble is that comparing is a game you will always lose (see chapter 8 where we discuss this problem in greater detail). Instead of playing that game, try this instead: The next time you find yourself comparing, say a prayer, thanking God for the gifts he has seen fit to give others and asking him to help you see more ways to cultivate and use your own. Ask God to help you see your own weaknesses as works-in-progress and your own strengths as a special calling to service and holiness.

If you answered TRUE to #2, here is a good penance for you: Assign one of those household tasks to someone else in the family. For example, if "only you" can fold the laundry properly, ask an older child to do it for you the next time. Then watch and do not correct. Say, "thank you," and nothing more. Finally, recognize that the laundry is indeed "folded"—and the world did not stop turning and the sky did not fall. At the end of this painful exercise, you can go back to folding all the laundry yourself if you want to, but do so with a renewed spirit of understanding that "perfection" in *doing* is not your goal in this life. Perfection in *loving* is.

Reflect on this quotation from Blessed Teresa of Calcutta and post it somewhere in your home where you will see it often:

> God doesn't ask that we succeed in everything, but that we are faithful. However beautiful our work may be, let us not become attached to it. Always remain prepared to give it up, without losing your peace.[2]

---

[2]   Jaya Chaliha and Edward Le Joly. *The Joy of Living: A Guide to Daily Living* (New York: Penguin, 2000), 334.

If you answered TRUE to #3, I have some bad news for you: The "right time" is never going to come. One of the most liberating things I ever did, several years ago, was to realize that the "right time" for me to begin writing professionally was never going to come. I was frustrated by the fact that hours of free time never suddenly opened up for me to begin writing.

I finally decided to "make do" with pockets of twenty and thirty minutes that opened up in my days and put the rest in God's hands. He has since blessed my trust in him many times over. Make a list of all the good things you are putting off because the timing is not yet "perfect"— taking up a new hobby, improving your prayer life, or taking a family trip. Now, look at your list, ask God to help you prioritize it, and then ... get started! I promise that God will bless and surprise you with the results.

If you answered FALSE to #4, spend a few moments reflecting on this Scripture passage:

> "Can a woman forget her sucking child, that she should have no compassion on the son of her womb?" Even these may forget, yet I will not forget you. Behold, I have graven you on the palms of my hands; your walls are continually before me.
>
> —Isaiah 49:15-16

Ask God to help you see that he loves you with a love that surpasses human understanding—far greater than even a mother's love. He has engraved you on the palm of his hand, and you are his precious child.

We all feel unlovable sometimes, but when we become parents ourselves, we have a helpful perspective for understanding the depth and strength of God's love. One of the most precious stages in toddler development, I think, is that stage when they begin to explore the world a bit, but yet every action and every experience of their days is anchored in their relationship with their mother. They immediately look for mommy whenever they experience a special joy (stacking a tower of blocks just so) or suffering (bumping their head on a table). No action or experience is complete until it is shared with Mom.

Since we are God's precious children, we too should consider no action or experience complete until we have shared it with him. God loves you, exactly as you are, and he wants you to bring it all to him. It is what we are made for. It is what love looks like. St. John Paul II reminds us:

> But the need for betrothed love, the need to give oneself to and unite with another person, is deeper and connected with the spiritual existence of the person. It is not finally and completely satisfied simply by union with another human being.[3]

The kind of self-giving love and union we mothers practice in our families and communities is a reflection of the greater communion we are called to have with our Creator. In love, on a cross, God gave us the gift of his very life. In love, through the Eucharist, he gives us the gift of himself in entirety—Body and Blood, Soul and Divinity. He waits for us to return with our complete gift of self. That kind of gift happens one small act of love at a time.

If you answered FALSE to #5, what is your natural response to failure instead?

Do you spend time beating yourself up over your weaknesses or immediately make a plan to improve upon them? Choose instead

---

[3]   Karol Wojtyla, *Love and Responsibility* (San Francisco: Ignatius Press, 1993), 253.

to make God part of your experience of failure. God loves you—beautiful, imperfect you—just as you are. He wants you to give all of yourself to him.

Do you know the Morning Offering? Do you pray it every day?

> *O Jesus through the Immaculate Heart of Mary,*
>
> *I offer you my prayers, works, joys,*
> *and sufferings of this day*
>
> *in union with the Holy Sacrifice of*
> *the Mass throughout the world.*
>
> *I offer them for all the intentions*
> *of your Sacred Heart:*
>
> *the salvation of souls, the reparation*
> *for sin, the reunion of Christians;*
>
> *and in particular for the intentions*
> *of our Holy Father this month.*
>
> *Amen.*

I especially love the part about offering up our "prayers, works, joys, and sufferings." You see? God wants it all. To help you keep this in mind, a small habit that is easy to start is to pray a Morning Offering every morning, and then repeat it throughout your day, especially during times when you fail or experience suffering of any kind. This small practice helps us to remember that we are God's precious children and that everything we experience, whether good or bad, success or failure, we can sanctify by offering back to him.

Chapter 5

Mothering and Smothering

"[A woman] finds herself ... in the very fact of giving herself 'through a sincere gift of herself.'"

—St. John Paul II[1]

Strength:

We are natural nurturers.

Weakness:

When we feel, speak, and care for others too much, we run the risk of smothering them.

---

[1]   John Paul II, General Audience, 6 February 1980; *GS* 24.

I recently dropped off my oldest son, Eamon, now seventeen years old, at a parish youth group event. As he walked away from the van, I sat behind the wheel for just a moment, watching him saunter toward the building. Mr. Cool was wearing sunglasses, a wide-brimmed cap, and Under Armour sneakers, but he couldn't fool me.

As he walked away, I saw the small boy who, for the first two years of his life, almost never left my arms. I recalled his pudgy, dimpled body and the "Li'l Sluggers" baseball cap he wore when he sat on the beach, watching waves and eating fistfuls of sand.

By the time Eamon was a year old, he could turn cartwheels and scale the curtains, but he still expected that I would pick him up whenever he demanded, which was all of the time. I became proficient at weeding the garden, cleaning the bathroom, and changing my clothes without ever once putting him down.

Eventually, I wound up at my doctor's office complaining of backache, occasional numbness, and sharp pains in my legs. He suggested I might have pinched a nerve and asked if I had been doing any heavy lifting.

"I carry a twenty-pound baby all day long," I told him.

He didn't get it. Reluctant to diagnose me with an acute case of motherhood, he wrote "sciatica" on my chart and sent me home with a dose of ibuprofen and a photocopied list of back-strengthening exercises.

As I was reminiscing about these things, my now-grown son stopped in his tracks on his way into the church, turned around, and trotted back to the van. "I forgot my sweatshirt!" he said as he opened the door. "Good thing you were still here."

He grabbed the sweatshirt, but before closing the van door looked at me quizzically. "Why *are* you still here?"

I did not tell him about his "smoochable" face and adorably pudgy arms. "Oh, I don't know," I answered innocently. "Just thinking, I guess."

Keeping Things Close

This is what we moms do. We watch. We think. We remember. We nurture. We love. We reflect. And we keep precious things close to our hearts. Because God made us to do exactly this. Mary knows this. One of my favorite passages from the New Testament is the one that describes Mary after the birth of Christ.

At that first Christmas all those years ago, the Blessed Mother did not run around the stable in a panic because she had no eggnog to offer the shepherds. Scripture tells us very little about anything Mary might have said or done at the Savior's birth, and this alone is telling.

> But Mary kept all these things, pondering them in her heart
> —Luke 2:19

Like Mary, we too "keep" the things of our motherhood—all the tiny details of those we love and care for—and reflect on them in our hearts. In this way, we give a great gift of love to our families. We notice their details, we memorize every dimple and curve of their tiny bodies, and, so thoroughly knowing them, we love them, inside and out, as only a mother can.

Mothering or Smothering?

Though we are built to notice small things and attend to them, the other part of being a loving mother is knowing when to stop nurturing. I recently read an essay where a forty-year-old man described going out to dinner with his mother. Worried about his vegetable intake, she grabbed his dinner roll and hid it in her purse until he had finished his peas. That is a bit much, wouldn't you say? Perhaps it is time to learn a new way to love your grown-up baby.

You might not be hiding grown men's dinner rolls in your pocketbook, but perhaps there are other ways you resist change in the ways you care for your children. A mother's heart can be such a delicate balance of conflicting emotion. One part of us wants our children to hurry up and wean, hurry up and potty train, hurry up and gain some independence already. And, yet, at the same time, another part of us wants them to never do any of those things and to remain exactly as they are forever. In fact, when the inevitable happens and they do gain some self-sufficiency, don't our hearts ache just a little bit at what feels like the ultimate betrayal?

As a consequence of original sin, our human experience is an imperfect one. On this side of heaven, we can never have or be all things perfectly. Growing up means giving up some childish things, some of which are precious, innocent, and beautiful to our parents who loved us from the start. While it is God's will that every human being should grow up and reach his or her full potential as an adult, it is natural for parents to mourn what is the very real loss of their children's smallness. The loss of childhood is real—it is the loss of innocence and of the small, beautiful creatures all of us once were. While we can recognize and appreciate the necessity (and beauty, too) of our children growing up and changing, it is OK to recognize what this growing up "costs" us. We all lose something precious and real as our children gain maturity and experience.

Teenaged Eamon, my formerly pudgy sand eater, breaks my heart a thousand ways a week. Would you believe me if I said that is just how it should be?

Like the time when he announced that he plans to call me "Mom" from now on, because "Mama" is too babyish and embarrassing? That only made me want to sob a little bit.

Or that time when I sat in the stands during one of his basketball games, and when Eamon's eyes landed on mine, he acknowledged my presence not with a wave, not with a big grin, but with a reserved and manly nod in my direction? Alrighty then. I will just swallow these mom-tears.

And swallow them we must. Do you hear me, moms? We must. There is nothing worse than a "smother-mother."

Perhaps the smother-mother in you does not manifest herself in mom-tears, but in a "hovering" habit when your kids go to school or play at the playground. Sometimes our growing children do need our guidance and support, but sometimes they need the "growing up" kinds of lessons they can only learn from being left to fend for themselves a little bit more regularly.

Another hard lesson for some of us smother-mothers to learn is that we are not always going to be the best person to meet all of our kids' needs. A grandmother who bakes or sews, a neighbor who can help with algebra, or a trusted aunt with whom our children feel comfortable expressing their fears and anxieties are gifts for which we should be grateful, not threats to our motherly vocations.

Sometimes Love Means Letting Go

It is hard to turn off the mom-machine at times. Clearly, God made us to mother. Our bodies, whether physically fertile or not, have wombs, breasts, and supple skin. We are meant to be receptive to life, to nurture life, and to be an incarnation of love to every human being, fruit of our womb or not, that God sees fit to place in our paths.

And yet a part of that nurturing, that love, and that receptivity is the very real and painful process of letting go. Our children and our families are not personal projects by which we will measure our successes and failures in this world. They are autonomous human beings, precious gifts that God only entrusts to our care for a temporary period of time.

Smother-mothers are frequent characters in cartoons and sitcoms. They are motherhood on steroids, and they make us laugh because they are so very real. And manipulating. And smothering. And even awful at times. On television or at the Thanksgiving dinner table, we know a smother-mother when we see her. We all know her—*and we are her*, to varying degrees.

Open to Gifts of Grace

Ironically, practicing our feminine gift of being open and receptive to others sometimes means putting up with some smother-mothering ourselves. When we succeed at this, the results are pure grace. When we fail, the results fall somewhat short of that.

"The juice! Don't forget the juice!" my mother-in-law, Dolores, called after me as I made my way down her front steps toward my car many years ago. Her anxious face appeared in the doorway as she thrust a half-gallon bottle of cranberry juice toward me.

I did not want the juice.

"Thank you," I answered weakly. I tucked the bottle under the passenger seat of the car and headed toward home—to the tiny apartment where my husband was waiting for me.

My husband. As a young bride, it still felt strange to put those two words together. In fact, the newness of my marriage was the reason I had trouble accepting gifts of cranberry juice from the in-laws.

Even as I was learning how to be a wife, Dan's mom was learning how to be the second woman in her son's life. And, like many of us, she did not let go easily. She still called to check on him, often did his laundry, and bought him all his favorite items at the grocery store, which included, of course, cranberry juice.

I was trying so hard to establish my own independence as a married woman that I resented my mother-in-law's well-intended involvement. Young, stubborn, and defensive, I saw an innocuous bottle of beverage as a threat to the autonomy of my marriage. Herein lies the lesson for all of us would-be smother-mothers. Our families absolutely do need us to love them and care for them, but at a certain point, that loving and caring is more about letting go than holding on.

Back then, I acquiesced. I brought the cranberry juice home to our apartment and placed it in the refrigerator where I resented its very presence. I do not remember if Dan drank it, but I do remember thinking of the juice weeks later, after Dan's mother suffered a debilitating stroke—because she never bought cranberry juice again.

Though Dolores lived for two more years before finally succumbing to cancer, she lost her memory and failed to recognize even her closest family members. My mother-in-law, a woman who had devoted her life to loving and caring for her family, became unable to care for herself. She, who had loved her own son so fiercely that she struggled with letting him go, never knew that she became a grandma.

In light of these events, resenting a bottle of cranberry juice seems more than just a little bit silly. And selfish. I was closed off to my mother-in-law's gift. I was closed off to grace. One of our greatest feminine strengths—that of receptivity and openness to other human beings—finds its first expression in the very essence of biological motherhood. The truth that biology reveals about our feminine genius is one that applies not only to biological motherhood, but also to the ways in which women are called to nurture, care for, and be receptive to all human beings.

> Motherhood involves a special communion with the mystery of life, as it develops in the woman's womb. The mother is filled with wonder at this mystery of life, and "understands" with unique intuition what is happening inside her. In light of the "beginning," the mother accepts and loves as a person the child she is carrying in her womb. This unique contact with the new human being developing within her gives rise to an attitude towards human beings—not only towards her own child, but every human being—which profoundly marks the woman's personality.[2]

---

[2]   *Mulieris Dignitatem* 18.

Although it has been many years since we lost Dan's mom, I still think of that cranberry juice on occasion. A few years ago, for example, my then-three-year-old, Raphael, somehow came to misunderstand the purpose of saying grace. No matter how mightily we tried, we failed to convince him that we should say grace to bless our food and give thanks to God. He believed that grace was a magic formula we used to cool off foods that were too hot to eat.

And so it was during one lunchtime that Raphael insisted upon saying grace twice over his steaming bowl of macaroni and cheese. When we were finished, and he found out the food was still hot, he demanded that we say grace again. Having indulged him once, though, I was weary of the game.

"We've already said grace two times," I told him. "Blow on your macaroni to cool it off."

He threw himself onto the floor in a rage.

"Grace! Grace! Grace!" he shouted as furious fists beat the wooden floor.

This behavior surely did not warrant special favors. I was ready to scoop up his screaming body and deposit him in another room, when his older brother intervened.

"I'll say grace again," Eamon offered.

Raphael brushed himself off, returned to his chair, sniffed righteously in my direction, and said grace with his brother.

As I listened to my boys' voices repeat the familiar words, I thought, *This is what grace is.* Undeserved and yet freely given, it is goodness and generosity poured out on the poorest, weakest of souls. This is the gift of grace we women are called to be. Not only in the ways we love our children, but also in the ways we are receptive to one another.

I whispered a prayer for the soul of a generous woman who loved my husband and me in ways I was once too childish to appreciate, and I thanked God for all of his gifts. Even the ones I have not asked for, and especially the ones I do not deserve.

Unique Children Have Unique Needs

We moms might be master nurturers and professional boo-boo kissers, but not all of our children are having it. Some of them have special needs or personalities that cause them to reject our care and affection at times. Some of them go through phases where they push us away and hurt our feelings. In these cases, love comes in the form of respecting boundaries and limitations to intimacy.

"What is he like?" I remember my mother asking in a phone call to the hospital just minutes after I delivered our fifth child, our third son, Stephen.

I anxiously studied his red and frowning face. "I think he's ... angry."

He might have had good reason to be angry. All those bright lights in the delivery room, all that noise and commotion surrounding his birth, all those feelings of hunger and variable body temperature we now expected him to handle on his own. Anger was an appropriate reaction to being born, and Stephen knew it.

Months later found me juggling my choleric child in one arm while I surfed the Internet with the other. "Dr. Google" offered one consistent diagnosis: "high-need infant."

Having a name for the particular brand of child I had been given offered some measure of relief, but little in the way of resolution. Like any good mother, I wanted to comfort my child. I wanted to soothe him until he was pacified, and I was unprepared for a child who preferred *not* to be pacified.

In the years following his "diagnosis," my high-need infant grew into a high-need toddler. My high-need toddler became a high-need preschooler. And these days, some might even call him a high-need eleven-year-old. Which I think is a politically correct way of saying ... demanding.

More than anything else, having a challenging child has taught me the value of recognizing my own limitations and the importance of loving others the way they need to be loved—which is not necessarily the way we would like to love them.

Loving Stephen means squelching my own desire to cover him with kisses and keeping a cautious distance instead, particularly when he is frustrated. Gentle coaxing works for some children when they are hurt or angry. Humor works with others. But Stephen? He needs to be left alone. The boy wants space to work out troubles on his own. And work them out he will.

Even moms without particularly challenging children can relate to the idea that each of their children are, in fact, individuals, who need to be loved in unique and individual ways. Ways that might make us uncomfortable because they might not always coincide with our own "love languages."

At one of Stephen's recent baseball games, he was on deck, warming up for his turn at bat. Before he stepped to the plate, I saw his eyes scan the sidelines intently until at last they landed on me. When our eyes met, he broke into a wide grin, and my heart swelled with the privilege of being there. With the joy of being this boy's mother—the one he looks for in the crowd.

Stephen does not need me to help him swing the bat. He does not need me to soothe him with sympathy. He just needs me to be there.

I can do that.

These days, I still keep a respectful distance when I see Stephen struggle to work his way through frustrating math problems or unpleasant chores at home. I watch in admiration as he plans business schemes to fund his desire for the latest video games and works hard to see them through. I now recognize that the other side of "demanding" is "determined" and "passionate."

Christ is determined and passionate, too. Just like my Stephen, the Lord does not do anything halfway. He does not do anything without meaning it in a big way. And he loves my passionate child even more than I do.

Are You a Smother-Mother?

Answer TRUE or FALSE to the following:

_____ 1. I sometimes dread the future, when my children will grow up and leave me.

_____ 2. I respect my children's needs for space and privacy in ways that are age-appropriate.

_____ 3. If I want to kiss my son, I am going to kiss my son, darn it.

_____ 4. I resist teaching my older children some basic household tasks (like laundry and meal preparation) because I want to be the one who does it for them.

_____ 5. I sometimes feel personally rejected by my children's growing independence.

If you answered TRUE to #1, take a number, sweetie. We all have mixed feelings when we think about an empty nest. Personally, I vacillate between uncontrolled elation and all-out panic at the thought of no more kids at home. Mixed feelings are normal, but sending mixed messages is not. Remember how we talked about overbearing sitcom smother-mothers? You are better than that. Pray for the grace to accept the changes that life brings, even the ones that involve the painful process of letting go and moving on.

Remind yourself of the people God made your children to be. Will they fulfill their lives' purpose and give glory to God by never moving out of your basement? Probably not.

Parenting author and expert, Dr. James Dobson, once said, "Parents who continue servitude as a child matures may be handicapping him or her for life. So a primary objective of parenthood is, quite simply, to work yourself out of a job."[3] Are you working yourself out of a job? To take the sting out of such a bittersweet assignment, we need to train ourselves not only to accept the inevitability of our children growing up, but all the little steps toward independence they will make to get there. Learn to see the joy in others becoming the people God means for them to be, and embrace your ever-changing role as a supporter, encourager, and cheerleader along the way.

If you answered FALSE to #2, log out of your son's Facebook account and put your daughter's diary down slowly. No, really. Think of a time in your younger life when you learned a painful but important lesson. Though the experience might have been a

---

[3]   Dr. James Dobson, "Growing Responsible Kids," paraphrasing Marguerite and Willard Beecher; DrJamesDobson.org.

painful one, do you think you would have been capable of learning the same lesson equally well through a textbook or a lecture?

One of the trickiest balances we mothers must learn to practice is that of figuring out which lessons our children are ready to learn for themselves and how we can be a source of support to them on the sidelines, even when we know they are going to make mistakes.

I was just kidding about the Facebook account and the diary, of course. Well, maybe just a little—there are definitely times when it is appropriate to stick our noses in our kids' "business," but it is equally important to recognize that, ultimately, our goal is to raise children who eventually are capable of having their own "business" and managing it well. Give your children the gift of helping them achieve independence.

If you answered TRUE to #3, I can empathize. Though similar things can happen with daughters, it surely hurts a mother's heart the day her son, of any age, rejects her hugs and kisses out of a newfound sense of manliness. We all know real men still smooch their moms, but sometimes love calls for a little bit of patience and understanding while your man-child figures this out for himself.

And it might not be just physical affection your children reject in an effort to assert their independence, either. It might be the brown-bag lunches you pack for school, the clothing you choose for them, or the violin lessons you pay for.

God sets a good example for us parents when it comes to selfless love. He loves us more than we can imagine, and yet he does not insist upon us accepting that love on his terms. He waits patiently—

always lovingly—for us to come to him, of our own will and in our own time.

Sometimes it will be best to stand your ground, but when you find yourself in a battle of wills with a growing child, it is important to consider the contentious issue prayerfully. Is this a place where you can afford to give your child some growing room? Yes? Then pray for the strength to follow God's example and love patiently while your child takes the lead.

If you answered TRUE to #4, I just want to give you a big old hug because that, my dear, is the definition of a loving mama—wanting to be *the one* who serves and cares for her children.

But let me remind you that there are other things to give your loved ones besides service. Important things, even. You can give them the feeling of accomplishment that comes from learning new skills. You can give them a sense of belonging by teaching them to contribute to family life. You can give them the lesson that God calls us all to serve others, and that the best way to practice service is with your own family, in your own home. You can give them the joy and satisfaction of caring for the needs of loved ones. You can give them the maturity that comes from having grown-up responsibilities. You can give them the gift of allowing them to love you and serve you in return.

This might mean teaching a disgruntled child to sort and fold laundry. It might mean enforcing acts of service in ways that elicit all manner of unpleasant reactions from your children. It might mean letting go of the idea that "only you" can love your family through acts of service. But you can do this. If you want to, you can still sneak in and make your son's bed after he leaves for school.

You can still make those special brownies your daughter loves. Just make sure your acts of service are balanced by time spent teaching your children to perform those same acts themselves.

If you answered TRUE to #5, think of Mary. Consider how hard it must have been for her to watch Jesus grow up, likely knowing that a bitter end was in store.[4] And yet she did it, because she knew this was God's will, for her, for the Son, and for all of mankind. While it is true that every little gain for a child is potentially a loss for his or her mother, we can retrain our hearts and minds to see our children's growing independence not as a loss for us, but as the accomplishment of our own goals.

Got him out of diapers? Good for you! Helped him pass the fifth grade? Bravo, Mom! Encouraged him through the SATs? Three cheers for you! Finally saw him graduate college, find a job, and marry the girl of his dreams? A job well done! You get the idea. Just fill in the details with your child's latest accomplishments.

Leaning on Mary in all of our motherly woes makes sense, but I think especially when we feel the pain of letting go. Let's pray together:

---

4   See Luke 2:34-35.

Dear Mary,

You loved Jesus with all your heart, and yet you knew when it was time to let him go. Help me to have the same loving heart for my children and to know, too, when it is time for me to let go. Help me to see the wisdom of God's plan and the beauty of his creation in my children's growing independence. When old ways must be put aside, help me to find new ways to love my children and support them in knowing, loving, and serving God in this world so that we can be happy together with him forever in the next.

Amen.

Chapter 6

Giving Till It Hurts ... Everyone

"[The] finding of oneself in giving oneself becomes the source of a new giving of oneself."

—John Paul II, General Audience, February 6, 1980

Strength:
We are naturally generous.

Weakness:
We forget to care for ourselves and wind up burned out and bitter.

I once cried over turtle food. Really, I did.

I can explain. Sort of.

I am sure every woman can relate to a busy day like the one I had not too long ago. I woke early to bring my eleven-year-old, Juliette, and twelve-year-old, Ambrose, to the pediatrician's office. I shook them from their beds, made breakfast, reset the bedroom alarm so that it would wake my husband on time for work, emptied the dishwasher, threw in a load of laundry, started the van so that it would warm up in the sub-zero February temperatures, picked up a pile of Matchbox cars that had been left on the floor from the previous evening, swept the floor, washed some dishes, wrote a note detailing morning chore assignments, and left the house.

Deep breath.

The kids' check-ups were lengthy but uneventful. On the way home, we stopped for gas, I made a few work-related phone calls, picked up the mail, and then raced to the grocery store for milk and bread.

I dropped off my two morning companions at home and honked the horn for my oldest son to come out of the house so that I could bring him to the school for a basketball team meeting. Driving home from the school, I answered a phone call from the kids at home. So-and-so was misbehaving, disobeying, and sneaking video games, they told me. "I am *not!*" I heard so-and-so shout in the background.

I told them to put the phone on speaker. Then, as I drove, I lectured all of them about the value of being cooperative, reminded them I would be home in five minutes, and hung up the phone.

Deep breath.

After I arrived home, I mediated all remaining arguments, made a few idle threats in the general direction of the preschoolers, and spent the next hours in general domestic management. That afternoon, as I arranged slices of bread in rows on the kitchen counter to prepare a pile of turkey sandwiches for lunch, my oldest daughter breezed into the room, reminded me that it was almost time for me to pick up her brother at the school and asked innocently, "Did you remember to get the turtle food?"

I walked into the bathroom, locked the door, and burst into tears.

I had forgotten the turtle food. Reptile nutrition had not yet risen to the top of my to-do list for the day. I had not ingested anything but a cup of coffee myself so far that day, and now that it was rushing past noontime, I was more interested in getting the kids' lunches made and having them finish their chores than in grocery shopping for turtles.

Poor Mi-shell. (That's the turtle.)

My tears were not so much about the stupid turtle food as my frustration with the fact that there always seemed to be something like the stupid turtle food to remind me that I was falling short; that I was not making it; that, as exhausted, distracted, and depleted as I was, I was still failing in some important way. I could give and give and give, I could do and do and do, and yet still it never was and never will be enough. My work will never be done. There will always be more responsibilities and dependent creatures than I can care for on my own, and I will never succeed at "doing it all."

Stupid turtle. Stupid me.

Deep breath. More tears. Stupid, stupid, stupid.

Seeing the Story

I don't suppose I have to tell you what the problem was. A *starving* person—a physically, emotionally, and spiritually *starving* person—cannot feed anyone else. It is easy for you to see that. You are reading my story. The trick is learning to see it in your own story.

Are you hungry? Are you starving? Do you feed yourself enough?

I am not talking about some kind of fast-food, drive-through void-filler—I am talking about feeding yourself real food. Soul food. Heart food. Real, nourishing food.

Do you do that? Most moms do not. I regret to say that too often I have been in the same boat.

A mother's need to feed herself starts early. At the very beginning of her motherhood, before she even knows she is pregnant, her body knows. And with or without her consent, the feeding begins. Immediately following fertilization, oxygen and nutrients are diverted from her body to nourish her developing baby.

Nobody asks. Nobody says thank you. A woman's body is built to do exactly this, and it just does it. More than that, though, our hearts and souls are built to feed and nourish others, too.

As St. John Paul II observes:

> Scientific analysis fully confirms that the very physical constitution of women is naturally disposed to motherhood—conception, pregnancy and giving birth—which is a consequence of the marriage union with the man. At the same time, this also corresponds to the psycho-physical structure of women. ... Motherhood as a *human* fact and phenomenon, is fully explained on the basis of the truth about the person. Motherhood *is*

linked to the personal structure of the woman and to the personal dimension of the gift: "I have brought a man into being with the help of the Lord" (Genesis 4:1). The Creator grants the parents the gift of a child. On the woman's part, this fact is linked in a special way to "a sincere gift of self." Mary's words at the Annunciation—"Let it be to me according to your word"—signify the woman's readiness for the gift of self and her readiness to accept a new life.[1]

The most important thing a pregnant woman can do to care for her developing baby in those early weeks is to eat well and rest. Likewise, the most important thing any mother can do for those in her care is to care enough for herself—physically, emotionally, and spiritually—to have ample stores from which to feed others.

God built us to give from our very selves. This natural generosity is a useful instinct and a special privilege in that it so beautifully reflects that generosity of God. We are most like our Creator when we give of ourselves fully. John Paul II described it this way:

Indeed, the Lord Jesus, when he prayed to the Father, "that all may be one ... as we are one" (John 17:21-22) opened up vistas closed to human reason, for he implied a certain likeness between the union of the divine Persons, and a unity of God's sons in truth and charity. This likeness reveals that man, who is the only creature on earth which God willed for itself, cannot fully find himself except through a sincere gift of self.[2]

A woman's natural inclination toward this kind of self-giving love is both a blessing and a burden. This especially draining aspect of our momnipotence requires that we care for ourselves in order to be able to care for others. Just as we would reprimand a pregnant

---

[1]   *Mulieris Dignitatem* 18.
[2]   *Gaudium et Spes* 24.

mother who skips meals and attempts to rearrange the living room furniture, so, too, should we reprimand ourselves when we ignore our own needs for physical, emotional, and spiritual rest and nourishment.

Nobody Needs Martyr Mom

To give without counting the cost is a beautiful concept, but in real life we do need to count the cost once in a while. Especially if the cost is our own health and happiness. A bitter, burned-out mother is not a pretty thing. She is anything but a gift to her family. I know this because I have been one.

I will never forget the evening my husband asked me to make him a special dinner. He was attempting to follow a new diet regimen and I had committed to supporting him in his healthy eating plan. What he did not know was that I had a pounding headache, the three youngest kids had been fighting all afternoon, I had a writing deadline early the next morning, and the kitchen was still a wreck from the dinner I had made for the kids just an hour earlier.

A mature person might have explained these circumstances to her husband, enlisted some help from him or the kids with cleaning up and disciplining the preschoolers, and worked out a plan for getting his special-request dinner made. Or, she might have asked if it would be OK to start the special diet the next night.

But I can only tell you what this immature person did. She pulled out the frying pan and slammed it onto the stovetop. She swept a pile of plates and cups into the kitchen sink with a clatter. She slapped a pound of chicken breast onto the cutting board and began hacking at it furiously with a knife.

When her husband arrived from the next room to see what the commotion was, she blinked back angry tears and hissed, "Don't worry. Nothing's wrong. You'll get your special dinner!"

Can you feel the love?

Before a Great Fall

Sometimes what we do under the guise of "serving our families" is really serving our own egos.

I have to do everything around here, we tell ourselves and others. *Because I am the only one who can do it right. Because no one else loves these kids as much as I do. Because I am the only one who knows how the baby likes her sandwiches cut, how to replace the toilet paper roll in the upstairs bathroom, and how to shake the vacuum cleaner just so to get it to start back up after a clog.*

And then, *Must I do everything around here?* we harrumph and sigh to ourselves as we reflect upon the fact that our poor, helpless families do not know which end of the broom is the sweeping one.

We also can get caught up in the idea that we are superwomen. We can nurse a baby, scrub a toilet, teach a kid fractions, and call the optometrist … all at the same time. Who else can do these things? Only a mom can.

To a certain extent that is true. It takes a woman's eye to notice and attend to many of the details that make a home run smoothly and that make the days more pleasant and productive. Details are our specialty. And we have a God-given ability to attend to many of those details at once.

I will be the first to admit that some mothers' multitasking and organizational skills are pretty amazing, and I have even impressed myself on occasion. But do any of us ever pause to wonder what all this *doing-doing-doing* is *doing-doing-doing* to our bodies? To our minds? To our souls?

Maybe we should pause to think about that.

Need to Feed

We have real physical and emotional needs for rest and nourishment. If we let our gift of natural generosity go unchecked, not only will we suffer, but our families will, too. It is not really generous to ignore our own needs for the sake of serving others because, in the end, those we intend to serve will bear the brunt of our own depression, burnout, anger, and resentment.

A pregnant or nursing mother knows that, as her baby grows, her own appetite increases to keep up with her child's needs. Give your life an honest assessment. Are you feeding many people with your time, energy, and attention? Is your own daily allotment of rest and nourishment enough to keep up with what you are dishing out?

Are you getting enough rest? Are you exercising? Are you eating well? Do you have time every day for prayer, social interactions, and quiet time alone if you crave it?

You need these things.

You have heard it before, but I am here to repeat it in an even more emphatic and demanding manner: *Feeding yourself is non-negotiable. You need these things.*

Well, that is easier said than done, you might be thinking. *You don't understand my life. I don't have a single minute to spare. My second-grader needs a tomato costume by Thursday, the baby has strep throat, I have work deadlines to meet, and do you really think the laundry is going to fold itself?*

Or fill in the blanks with your own life circumstances, whatever they may be—work, school, or family-related. The details differ, but many of us have that same feeling in the end: We are maxed out. We are overwhelmed. We have nothing to spare.

I get it. But guess what? That "maxed out" feeling is not an excuse to neglect yourself. In fact, just the opposite is true. That "maxed out" feeling is exactly what tells you that you need to take better care of yourself.

Let's find out just how hungry you are with a quick quiz.

Are You Starving?

Answer TRUE or FALSE to the following:

_____ 1. I do the lion's share of the housework, even
though I have a husband and older children who
are able to pitch in.

_____ 2. I have my own hobbies and interests and the
time to pursue them.

_____ 3. I justify my impatience with family members
by telling myself I am tired from all that I do for
them.

_____ 4. I have time to pray every day.

_____ 5. I sometimes get angry when my husband (or
anyone else) makes suggestions for lightening
my workload.

If you answered TRUE to #1, you might have too much pride wrapped up in the idea of "doing it all" yourself. I would encourage you to experiment with the fine art of something I like to call "delegating and walking away."

Here is a little tough love for you: If you died tomorrow, your family would miss *you*, not the sparkling toilet bowls. Give them more of you—the *real* you—by recognizing and accommodating your own limitations.

Let go of the ridiculous, self-aggrandizing notion that you are the only person who can do things properly. Delegate some household duties to the kids. (I promise they will not die, and their future spouses will thank you). Let your husband win your affections with an occasional well-washed sink full of dishes. If finances allow, hire someone else to do some of the housework. And then (here is the important part), *walk away*.

Cross the delegated chores off your to-do list and forget about them. Take a walk. Breathe some fresh air. Find a hobby. Whatever you do, do *not* hang around inspecting and clicking your tongue over other people's shoulders.

If you answered FALSE to #2, read these words out loud: THIS IS NOT OK.

Very few mothers have time to pursue *all* of their own interests, but every one of us can make time to pursue *some* of them. Ask yourself, and if you come up blank, ask God, "What kinds of things refresh and invigorate me? What kinds of activities make me feel good about myself?"

Listen to the answers, and then make the time to do some of those things. You can "make" the time by not only "delegating and walking away," but by practicing another fine art I like to call "letting some things go."

Even once you get good at delegating, it is a simple fact of family life that there still will be days when not everything gets done according to your standards. You will discover a sink filled with dirty dishes at 11:00 PM. You will not get around to mopping the sticky kitchen floor before your mother-in-law drops by. The dog will vomit a partially eaten rodent onto the couch just minutes before the entire family must leave the house for a wedding. (Please do not tell me I am the only person this has ever happened to).

Prepare yourself now, and you will be ready to pull through with grace and style when the inevitable happens. Here is what to do when it does: (1) Take a breath. (2) Ask yourself, "Will this matter a hundred years from now?" or, "Might this make a funny story when all is said and done?" (3) Laugh and let it go.

If you answered TRUE to #3, you might need to reflect on the fact that no mother ever lay on her death bed, surrounded by her loving family members and wished she had sighed and harrumphed at them more often. Do you really want your family to feel loved? If so, then doing everything yourself—especially if it makes you impatient, resentful, or passive-aggressive—is not the way to go.

I once saw a TV commercial for paper plates that promoted their product as family-friendly. "Make it a Dixie day," the announcer suggested, as we watched happy scenes of mothers snuggling on the couch, playing games, and reading books with their children. I am not a wisdom snob. I recognize perceptive insights even when they come from the mouths of paper product manufacturers. Wouldn't it make your kids feel loved if they were able to spend more time with you—a relaxed and happy you—even if it meant leaving the laundry unfolded on occasion? Ask your children or your husband what things you do that make them feel most loved. Their answers might surprise you. Cross off some of the stuff they *do not* say and add their answers to your to-do lists instead.

If you answered FALSE to #4, you probably should rethink your daily routines (see numbers 1-3 above), but you also might need to rethink your prayer habits. If you put off prayer until you can find or make the right amount of time to "do it right," it might be decades before God hears from you.

A busy life spent living out an active vocation to motherhood should not be an obstacle to a Christ-centered life. Daily prayer can mean a Morning Offering while you get dressed, a Hail Mary for each child as he or she heads off to school, a few minutes with a favorite prayer book at lunchtime, candid conversation with God while you fold the laundry, or hymns sung while doing the dishes. The key is to practice the habit of turning your heart and mind to God throughout your day. The more you do this, the easier it will become. Think of yourself as a precious child of God, turning toward your Father in all the joys and sorrows of your day. Because guess what? That is just what you are.

If you answered TRUE to #5, you clearly have people in your life who care about you and want to help you take care of yourself. Your job is simple, but not easy: *Let them.*

It is pride that makes us cling to the idea of rejecting help and "doing it all" ourselves, and that pride can only hurt you and your loved ones in the end. Here's a prayer to help you:

Dear God,

Help me to let go of pride and vanity so that I might become a humble instrument of your love to all those I want to serve. Help me to accept the gift of grace you give me each day, to let go of perfectionism, and to embrace the ways you would have me serve my family and community. Help me to be a good steward of my time, energy, and attention, using each of these resources to feed myself enough so that I am better able to love and serve others in your name.

Amen.

Chapter 7

Do What You Are Doing

"Accept the duties which come upon you quietly, and try to fulfill them methodically, one after another. If you attempt to do everything at once, or with confusion, you will only cumber yourself with your own exertions, and by dint of perplexing your mind you will probably be overwhelmed and accomplish nothing."

—St. Francis de Sales[1]

Strength:
We are master multitaskers.

Weakness:
When we do too many things at once, the quality of our work and relationships can suffer.

---

[1]   *Introduction to the Devout Life*, chapter X.

One of the most popular things I ever tweeted was, "I just broke up a wrestling match while stuffing a turkey and making a dental appointment. I am mom, hear me roar."

I think people really responded to it because they saw themselves (or their own wives or mothers) in that kind of randomly ridiculous multitasking. Who else but a mother would even attempt to do all those things at once? Families expect this kind of multitasking from moms, and more often than not, we deliver. I am guessing that the following everyday conversations heard in my house might sound similar to those heard in yours.

"Mo-ooooom! ... Where is my G.I. Joe ammunition belt, how do you spell rhinoceros, can you tie my shoes, the baby's throwing pancakes again, are you done with the laundry yet, Mrs. Jenkins is on the phone, someone left rocks in the sink, I need a ride to baseball, what's a greatest common factor, there are no clean spoons, what's for lunch, can you braid my hair, and the golf team needs a dozen pizzas today by 5:30."

Nobody needs to tell a mom that she thinks about and attends to many things at once, but there has been some scientific study and discussion of the differences between the sexes with regard to multitasking. In her book, *The Female Brain,* Dr. Louann Brizendine goes so far as to assert that women's brains are physically different from men's brains.[2] A 2006 study from Missouri Western State University notes:

> Women have a larger corpus callosum. The corpus callosum is the
> area of the brain that handles communication between the two
> hemispheres. It is responsible for synthesizing the information

---

[2]   See Louann Brizendine, MD, *The Female Brain* (New York: Harmony, 2007).

from the left and right side of the brain. In women, the corpus callosum is wider than that of men's brains, which might enable the two sides to communicate better with each other. This is a theory as to why women might multitask more efficiently.[3]

Like Waffles and Spaghetti

It is just a fact that men and women process information and activity differently. We need only attempt to communicate and interact with a member of the opposite sex to find out how very differently we sometimes function.

Authors Bill and Pam Farrel, in their book, *Men Are Like Waffles, Women Are Like Spaghetti: Understanding and Delighting in Your Differences,* make what I think is an accurate (and amusing) observation about differences between the sexes. They begin by explaining the ways in which a man's brain, like a waffle, is compartmentalized:

> Men are like waffles. ... What we mean is that men process life in boxes. If you look down at a waffle, you will see a collection of boxes separated by walls. The boxes are all separate from each other and make convenient holding places. This is typically how a man processes life. Our thinking is divided up into boxes that have room for one issue and one issue only. The first issue of life goes in the first box, the second issue goes in the second box, and so on. The typical man lives in one box at a time and one box only.[4]

The Farrels go on to explain the very different, and more "spaghetti-like," approach of the female brain:

3   Brandy R. Criss, "Gender Differences in Multitasking" (Missouri Western State University, 2006). http://clearinghouse.missouriwestern.edu/manuscripts/815.

4   Bill and Pam Farrel. *Men Are Like Waffles, Women Are Like Spaghetti: Understanding and Delighting in Your Differences* (Eugene, OR: Harvest House, 2007), 10-11.

In contrast to men's waffle-like approach, women process life more like a plate of pasta. If you look at a plate of spaghetti you notice there are lots of individual noodles that all touch one another. If you attempted to follow one noodle around the plate, you would intersect a lot of other noodles, and you might even switch to another noodle seamlessly. That is how women face life. Every thought and issue is connected to every other thought and issue in some way. Life is more of a process for women than it is for men. ... Because all her thoughts, emotions, and convictions are connected, she is able to process more information and keep track of more activities.[5]

In short, while there certainly are exceptions, most women are master multitaskers, and most men, even if they are very good at multitasking, do so with less ease than a woman does. Men typically do one thing at a time, while it would appear that we women are pre-programmed with the ability to do many things at once.

The Cost of Doing

We take multitasking for granted. We can do it. Our lives often require that we do it. We should just do it, right?

Not so fast. While some kinds of multitasking are fine and helpful, we need to pause now and then to consider this: What does all of our "doing" cost us? What price are we paying for our busy-ness— physically, emotionally, and spiritually?

There is value in slowing down and living simply, just one moment at a time. We need to pause more often to recognize that.

---

[5]   Bill and Pam Farrel, *Men Are Like Waffles, Women Are Like Spaghetti: Understanding and Delighting in Your Differences* (Eugene, OR: Harvest House, 2007), 10-11.

Do What You Are Doing

Years ago, my online friend Alicia Van Hecke introduced me to what wound up being a life-changing concept. She shared a simple phrase in Latin (because she is cultured like that) that really made me pause: *age quod agis.*

What does it mean? It means *do what you are doing.* That's all. It is that simple. Simple, I say, but not easy. As every mother knows, sometimes it can be very hard to slow down and simply "do what you are doing," one thing at a time.

I sometimes manage to sneak away for a little while and attend Mass or Adoration by myself. There, in silence with no distractions, I can become frustrated because my brain simply spins. So unaccustomed to silence and inactivity, my "busy" self rushes in to fill the void.

What should I make for dinner? I find myself thinking. *I wonder if there will be time to stop at the store on the way home. Was I supposed to call my mother back? I need to remember to buy wrapping paper before the birthday party this weekend. My nails sure could use a coat of polish. Is it cold in here? ... What am I doing here, anyway? Oh yes, JESUS! There you are! Here I am, paying attention!*

It is embarrassing the number of times this cycle will repeat itself over the course of an hour. There I am, not doing what I am doing.

We do not do this just at church, though. Distracted thinking can happen anywhere and at any time. Take a moment now and ask yourself this question: "Do I look my children in the eye when they speak to me? Or do I grunt at them while I am focused on other things?"

I am not asking this question in order to inspire guilt trips. We are all busy and distracted some of the time. I am asking because I think we should all consider the positive effect that giving ourselves permission to do just one thing at a time can have on our mental health and our relationships.

Letting Go

I say "give ourselves permission to do one thing at a time" deliberately, because that is precisely what we need to do. No matter what worthy thing we are doing, there is some voice inside of us that nags, reminds, and calls us to concentrate on some other worthy thing. Then, because they are all worthy things, we feel guilty if we ignore the nagging.

If you have trouble just "doing what you are doing," ask yourself, in moments where you are tempted to distraction, "Does my vocation require that I be [fill in the blank here: chopping vegetables, tying a toddler's sneaker, shopping for groceries, feeding a baby, driving a carpool, talking to my teenager] right now?"

No matter how small the task, if the answer to that question is yes, then it is enough. There, in that moment, you are giving 100 percent of yourself to the work God calls you to, and you do not need to be thinking about or doing anything else.

Repeat after me: "This is enough. I am busy enough. I am doing enough."

Feeling Accomplished

As I discovered when I first found myself challenged by the idea of *age quod agis*, it takes a great leap of faith to trust that we are being faithful to our calling, even when we are not completing the 237 things on our to-do list this week. It is just so very nice to have the tangible sense of accomplishment and security that comes from crossing off the items on that list, even if it is only a mental list.

Some seasons of our lives are just not conducive to those kinds of tangible accomplishments, though. Ask any parent of a toddler. By the end of the day, merely having the house look sort of like it did in the morning—all the books in the bookcase, all the pots and pans in the cabinets, and all the toilet paper on the roll—is a very big accomplishment. But it is often hard to see that kind of accomplishment from the outside.

We are meant to keep a much bigger picture in mind than our to-do lists. We need to determine the value of our days in terms of whether or not they brought us and our families closer to heaven. We must change the questions we ask ourselves.

Ask yourself: *Does my vocation require that I be scraping cemented oatmeal from the high-chair tray right now?* Or, *Does my vocation require that I get up before the sun to pack lunches and make breakfast before forty minutes of driving because today is my turn for the school carpool?*

Answer to both questions: Yes, it does. And it is enough.

Ask yourself: *Did I move myself and my family closer to heaven today?*

Answer: Yes, I did. And that means it was a good day.

Simplicity and Trust

Our children are an inspiring example of the peace that comes from leaving the multitasking to others and concentrating on doing just one thing at a time. Have you ever watched a child at play? While he pushes Matchbox cars along the carpet, he is not worrying about whether or not his room is messy, or if he should be playing ball with his friends. He is living in the moment, doing what he is doing, and he is actually glorifying God in the process.

Inspiration and example comes from other, unexpected places as well. A few years ago, when my husband told me he had hired a recovering drug addict to do some carpentry work in the house, I was not sure what to expect. The man needed work, my husband explained; he came highly recommended by a close friend, and he could get the job done as quickly as we liked.

And that is how I came to meet Dan. Tall, skinny, and shaky, he entered our home and gazed admiringly at its wood interior. When my husband introduced us, Dan turned his head slightly sideways, and his eyes darted from somewhere above my head down to his own weathered work boots.

"Nice to meet you," he mumbled. "Good morning."

Then he familiarized himself with the location of the lumber and saws, pulled out his tape measure, and got to work.

With his long, gray ponytail pulled through the back of a greasy baseball cap, tattooed arms, and swarthy skin, Dan did not look at all like the kind of person who normally visits our home. The children, who had been instructed to stay out of "Mr. Dan's" way, watched him from a cautious distance. Even the dog, normally an obnoxious pest with either too much barking or too much affection when company calls, observed him coolly from the front doorway.

When I prepared lunch for him the first day and pressed him for his preferences—*White or wheat? Mustard or mayo?*—he just shrugged. Despite my invitation to join us at the dining room table, "Mr. Dan" took his lunch plate and a tall glass of Diet Coke to a lawn chair he pulled into the shade at the edge of the woods behind the house. There, he ate his lunch and smoked cigarettes, carefully extinguishing the butts and depositing them in his fanny pack before returning to work.

As awkward as Dan was at making small talk in my kitchen, he was at home with wood and work. Noise filled the house and sawdust flew through the air as he sawed, hammered, drilled, and chiseled. He trimmed out doorways and routered windowsills with precision. He produced perfect corners and smooth edges in record time.

When my husband arrived home from work hours later and pronounced the work "perfect," Dan swallowed a smile and squirmed with pleasure at the sound of praise. A hard life had turned this former motorcycle gang member into something so pure and plain that even his hardened exterior could not hide it.

I want something as pure and plain as that.

I know at least one of the reasons God sent Dan to work in my home that week. How else to get this distracted mother of eight to compare the details of her days—the intangible and yet important work of raising souls to know, love, and serve God—with those of a broken man who simply works and simply trusts, doing one simple thing at a time?

Dan has an enviable ease of faith. In a conversation with my husband, he revealed some near-misses he survived while living a wild life on the edge of destruction.

"I'm not sure who it is," he said, "but someone's watching out for me. I've got some kind of an angel."

Throughout my life, God has showered me with grace upon grace, gift upon gift, and yet I still struggle to believe sometimes. Is God really there? Does he truly know me and love me? Does he care at all about the details of my days? Does it matter if I am faithful in these small things? Does anyone notice or even care?

Like Dan, I want to keep my head down and focus on my work. But most of all, I want to trust. I want to know that whatever kinds of mistakes I might have made in the past, God loves me and wants what is best for me. I want to believe that I can be faithful to my calling one small task at a time, just doing what I am doing, even if the accomplishments are hard to see from the outside.

After his departure, Dan's lawn chair sat empty at the edge of the woods. Mr. Dan's work at my home was done. But the lessons I learned from him were just beginning.

Are You Too Busy?

Answer TRUE or FALSE to the following:

_____ 1. I make room in every day for a little bit of quiet.

_____ 2. I do things like check my email, check my phone, and turn on the TV without even thinking.

_____ 3. I feel guilty and/or anxious when I sit still for any length of time.

_____ 4. I make a habit of savoring small things like a child's laugh, a warm cup of coffee, or a sunny porch on a regular basis.

_____ 5. I give myself permission to do just one thing— even seemingly small, insignificant things—at a time.

If you answered FALSE to #1, now is the perfect time to get yourself in the habit of slowing down and practicing the fine art of just *being*. It does not have to be complicated, and you do not have to make it "official" prayer time. You can get up ten minutes before the kids do or sneak into the bathroom and lock the door behind you.

One trick I use is to make sure I spend some time outdoors every day. This can be a bit of a challenge, because I live in New Hampshire (also known as "the Frozen Tundra" six months of every year). Even if you spend just five minutes standing on the front steps or in the driveway, though, there is nothing quite like getting outdoors if your goal is to put some distance between yourself and ringing phones, buzzing laundry machines, and screeching children. God made the natural world for us to live in and enjoy. Make sure you are connecting with it on a regular basis—your efforts will be rewarded with a renewed sense of peace, even when you must return to the chaos.

If you answered TRUE to #2, you are exactly like most Americans, addicted to toys and noise. Here is something to consider, though: God might have something to say to you right now, but he is waiting patiently for you to be ready and open to hearing it. He will not attempt to compete with the latest episode of *Downton Abbey*.

You might find it helpful to calm your multitasking brain by setting aside specific "electronic-free" times. Cell phones, tablets, and computers can be used to talk or text, chat or email, without making a sound. But we need to take into account the kind of "noise" the useless distraction of these seemingly harmless bits of technology makes in our brains. Hide the remote, close the laptop, and put the cell phone away for a set period of time every day. Your frazzled brain will thank you for it.

If you answered TRUE to #3, you will want to read carefully these words from Father Benedict Groeschel:

> Enjoy what's going on while it's going on. If you go to the supermarket, enjoy it. Don't make it drudgery. Talk to the cashier. Speak to the people at the fruit counter. Chat with a neighbor. Try to get to know people, get them to talk to you, and make your passage through life pleasurable. ... Slow down. Smell the flowers as you go by, and then you won't need too much of this world's goods. Enjoy your work and you won't need too much time off. Enjoy being at home and you won't have to go away so much. Many people are intemperate because they are miserable and suffering. Their life is a big long misery, so they decide to brighten it up with mountains of potato chips. They're addicted to potato chips or sweets or even beer. Look at your own intemperateness and see if unhappiness is causing it.[6]

In other words, *age quod agis*. Do what you are doing. No excuses. Start now.

If you answered FALSE to #4, let's talk about baby books. Most of us are familiar with baby books—those cute little journals where you are supposed to carefully paste a tiny lock of your child's hair and record precious moments like taking first steps and eating a first ice-cream cone. It seems there's always someone at a baby shower who thinks it is a good idea to burden the new mother with one of these guilt-inducing items.

---

[6]   Benedict J. Groeschel, *The Virtue Driven Life* (Huntington, IN: Our Sunday Visitor, 2006), 83.

If you have baby books and they are meticulously filled out, you have my eternal admiration. But if you have baby books and they are sitting untouched in a cardboard box in your bedroom closet where they cause you pangs of guilt when you accidentally lay eyes on them while looking for the Christmas lights, come on over for coffee, my friend. You are my kind of mom.

The idea behind baby books, though, is one I think we can all appreciate. We think we will not forget the baby years, but then we do. Early childhood is a hectic business, after all, and in the end, our memories of those early months—years, even—do grow a little fuzzy around the edges.

The good news is that we all have access to something even better than baby books. It is called "right now." Whether your children are still babies or not, regard this moment as God's gift to you. Savor it. Give glory to God and do justice to your calling by doing what you are doing and fully experiencing it. Live it fully. Enjoy it completely. No excuses.

If you answered FALSE to #5, ask God to help you slow down and "single-task" instead of multitasking through your days. Here is a prayer to get you started:

Dear God,

Sometimes my head spins with the number of things that I must do, worry about, and keep up with. Help me to see that you never demand accomplishments, but only faithfulness and love, even in small things. My world is made up of those small things. Give me grace to make every moment of my days a gift to you. When I forget and become distracted, remind me that my heart will not rest until it rests in you. Anchor my heart in you, Lord. As I go about the duties of my day, give me the peace that can only come from you.

Amen.

Chapter 8

Devilish Details

"Parents' respect and affection are expressed by the care and attention they devote to bringing up their young children and providing for their physical and spiritual needs."

—Catechism of the Catholic Church *2228*

Strength:
We notice the details.

Weakness:
When we notice the details in others' lives, we can become discouraged and distracted from our own vocations.

Do you ever compare yourself to other women?

Most of us do. It is OK to admit it. Honesty is the first step toward intervention, and intervention is the first step toward breaking the destructive habit of self-loathing that too many of us engage in when we come out on the losing side of a comparative exercise.

Why, for instance, when we have the good fortune of meeting a fabulous new friend—some lovely lady with an immaculate home and a brood of well-behaved children who play classical violin and recite the Gettysburg Address on cue—why do we come away from this new friendship feeling just a little bit bad about ourselves?

Why, for example, do we see another woman's impressive community involvement, successful husband, or amazing culinary skills and beat ourselves up for not having accomplished the same things in our own lives? Or worse yet, pick apart others' talents or accomplishments in an envious attempt to diminish them?

Why do we women do this?

I certainly am not immune. One year, not too long ago, in mid-December I received one of *those* Christmas cards in the mail. With one of *those* family Christmas letters tucked inside. And one of *those* family photos, too.

You know the kind I'm talking about. The "perfect family" kind.

The mother of this particular family looked at least a couple of years younger and certainly a few pounds thinner than she had in the previous year's card. Her hair and makeup were flawless. The father was dashing, too (and quickly scaling the corporate ladder, the family letter would soon inform me). And the children? Why, these glowing little cherubs were perfectly polished and poised. Even the dog, an elegantly groomed golden retriever, posed with pristine paws crossed "just so" for our admiring eyes. (I think he was stuffed.)

The perfection of it all was painful to behold.

It did not help that my own family happened to be knee-deep in the throes of a stomach virus at the time. I was contemplating canceling Christmas dinner, never mind pulling off a photo shoot and a perfectly written Christmas letter. Besides, you could have supplied me with an unlimited budget, a fleet of designers, and a team of professional photographers, and still I could not have achieved what that woman had managed, seemingly effortlessly, with her own flawless family in her own luxurious living room.

I compared. And I came out pathetic. And then, as pathetic people are wont to do, I decided to wallow in my misery.

Now, misery *does* love company, and fortunately for me, when I want to wallow, I have my choice of three amazing sisters who generally will indulge my wallowing at the drop of a hat. I dialed my youngest sister's number and began my whine-fest before she had even finished saying hello.

"*Whyyy* is my life such a mess? *Whyyy* is this woman *sooo* perfect?" I moaned into the phone.

All of my sisters are wise and sensible women. I am blessed that they love me for who I am, but are unafraid to give me an occasional wake-up call when I need one. Or whine for one, as the case may be.

Annoyingly, on this particular day, my youngest sister was all sense and business.

"Do you really think she has a perfect life?" she interrupted me mid-whine. "I mean, seriously perfect?"

"I don't *knoooooow*," I whined.

"Come on," my sister persisted. "Her toddler never bites the baby?"

Which made me pause. Because of course Mrs. Perfect's toddler bites the baby. Or does something like that. Every family has their share of kids who wet their pants in the pew at church and decorate the walls with a Sharpie. We just don't put *that* in our Christmas cards.

Inside, Outside, Upside Down

It is important to remember that we are all editors. All the details others see and know about us are ones we have chosen share.

Now, this is not entirely a bad thing. I am certainly not arguing that more of us should "keep it real" by airing our personal and familial dirty laundry for public view. But this is an important concept to keep in mind. We see what other people choose to share about themselves, and what they choose to share, for the most part, will be their very best, their most flattering details, and those things they are most proud of. These are their *exterior* details.

But we all know—in brutally honest and embarrassingly intimate detail—our own *interiors*. That is where the dirt lives, isn't it?

It is not fair to compare our own insides with others' outsides. The inside stories of my marriage will never stack up to the outside images of other families I know. The interior details of my children's weaknesses, failures, and mistakes will never shine in the light of the exterior accomplishments of other people's children. And, I have come to realize, my own flawed and struggling interior will never match up to some other woman's perfect Christmas card.

It is not fair to put that kind of pressure on our husbands and children. It is not fair to demand that kind of perfection from ourselves. When we misuse our gift for details and engage in this kind of comparison, we come away feeling anything but momnipotent.

Women have an eye for details. We notice small things about others and ourselves. We cannot help it. God made us this way. This is a great feminine gift that every woman can use in service to others, whether she is married or a biological mother, or not. Let's take a look at how Mary can help us to see the positive, grace-filled ways God intends for us to use this feminine strength.

Seeing Mary in the Details

Mary noticed details. In the infancy narratives in the Gospel of St. Luke, for example, how could Luke have known all the precious and beautiful details he shares about the birth of Christ? He was not there, but Mary was. As the Gospel tells us, Mary "kept all these things, pondering them in her heart" (Luke 2:19). She stored them away, so that the entire world might benefit later from her insight into the early life of Jesus Christ. What an amazing gift her feminine strength enabled her to give us all!

In the Gospel story about the wedding at Cana, our Blessed Mother offers us another exceptional example of feminine note-taking:

> On the third day there was a marriage at Cana in Galilee, and
> the mother of Jesus was there; Jesus also was invited to the
> marriage, with his disciples. When the wine failed, the mother
> of Jesus said to him, "They have no wine." And Jesus said to her,
> "O woman, what have you to do with me? My hour has not yet
> come." His mother said to the servants, "Do whatever he tells
> you (John 2:1-5).

They were out of wine. Not that big a deal, right? Jesus certainly did not seem to think it very noteworthy. "How does your concern affect me?" he asked, but Mary, his mother, perfect model of grace-filled womanhood, noticed all the details and was patiently persistent.

"Do whatever he tells you," she told the servants.

Mary was womanly perfection, conceived without sin and perfectly aligned with God's will every moment of her life. In this one, small episode, we find our first taste of Mary's perfect example of feminine sensitivity to small details.

Think of that wedding party. It was probably a noisy celebration with all kinds of male and female guests who were oblivious to the hosts' embarrassing predicament. But Mary noticed. The hosts realized that they had run out of wine. It was a socially awkward position, perhaps, but not a crisis of life-or-death proportions. But this is just what a woman can excel at—noticing the needs of others, however small, and quietly bringing them to the attention of those who can do something to help.

What Only Mom Can See

At my son Stephen's recent baseball game, another one of the moms in the bleachers was attending the game with her teenaged son while her younger son was on the mound, pitching. Poorly.

"I wish he wouldn't put so much pressure on himself," she sighed, frowning.

After her son threw two more balls, I saw her nudge her older son. His eyes were glued to the screen of his cell phone as his flashing thumbs worked the device's keypad.

"Pay some attention to your brother," she told him. "When he looks over here, maybe you could give him a wave or something. Just let him know you're watching."

The teen sighed and rolled his eyes, but obliged his mother's request. The next time the nervous pitcher looked toward the bleachers, his eyes met his older brother's. Big brother gave little brother a smile, a wave, and a thumbs-up. Little brother broke into a wide grin and waved back before returning to his pitching with renewed confidence.

Our sensitivity and attention to detail sometimes enable us to love and serve others from the sidelines in ways that no one else can. We might not meet all of our children's needs perfectly all the time, but we are pretty darn good at identifying needs—however small— and guiding others toward serving and loving well.

Sometimes the "others" we guide and teach in this subtle way are our own husbands, the fathers of our children. Did you know that your man needs you not only to remind him to call his Aunt

Mildred on her eighty-second birthday, but that he also relies on you to demonstrate for him at times how to be an engaged and loving father, brother, son, and friend? Not in a domineering, bossy way, of course, but with gentle nudges toward loving interaction.

St. John Paul II recognized this feminine strength and responsibility when he wrote:

> It is commonly thought that *women* are more capable than men of paying attention *to another person,* and that motherhood develops this predisposition even more. The man—even with all his sharing in parenthood—always remains "outside" the process of pregnancy and the baby's birth; in many ways he has to *learn* his own *"fatherhood" from the mother.* One can say that this is part of the normal human dimension of parenthood, including the stages that follow the birth of the baby, especially the initial period. The child's upbringing, taken as a whole, should include the contribution of both parents: the maternal and paternal contribution. In any event, the mother's contribution is decisive in laying the foundation for a new human personality.[1]

If you have ever suffered a miscarriage, it is likely that you have experienced this very real difference between the sexes. To a woman, the reality of a new baby's life begins the moment she dreams of him or her, the moment she sees two tiny pink lines and becomes aware of a tiny soul's presence within her womb. She loves. She connects. She bonds. By sharing her physical self with her unborn child, she develops an intimate and deeply connected relationship with this tiny being that even the most loving father could never replicate.

---

[1]   *Mulieris Dignitatem* 18.

The loss of such a connection, however early in the process, is a deep and wounding experience for most women. Although men suffer by seeing us suffer and often are attached to the idea of a baby, for them the loss is exactly that—the loss of an idea, a connection that they accept and understand, but do not yet *feel* in the same way we do.

When it comes to the details of love and relationships, women are natural-born leaders. We sweat the small stuff. Thank God for good women who do.

Do you use your gift of noticing the details in ways that foster love and build relationships, or do you use your gift to compare yourself to others and beat yourself up for falling short of perfection? Let's take a quick quiz.

Are Details Your Downfall?

Answer TRUE or FALSE to the following:

_____ 1. One of my first instincts while in the presence of other women is to "stack myself up" against them, quickly determining if I am above or below them in terms of beauty, brains, material goods, or other gifts.

_____ 2. I sometimes compare my husband unfavorably to other women's husbands, even if only in my own mind.

_____ 3. I take seriously my responsibility to love others and lead them to love, especially in small ways.

_____ 4. I recognize that God has given me my particular marriage and my particular children because he knows what is best for me.

_____ 5. I recognize that my talent for loving my husband and children in small ways is a great gift.

If you answered TRUE to #1, join the club. And then let's make a pact to stop doing this to ourselves and others. It can be tempting to seek self-worth in human relationships and competition, especially when a secular society encourages us to do exactly that.

When we compare ourselves to others, whether as a means of building ourselves up or putting ourselves down, we take God out of the equation. We fail to recognize the unique gift that each of us is to our families, our communities, and our Church.

God might call each of us to a vocation of marriage and motherhood, but the ways in which he does that are as varied as the women he calls.

I once heard this temptation to compare ourselves explained in terms of "horizontal" and "vertical" relationships. Are you seeking self-worth and affirmation in horizontal relationships, carefully watching the ways in which you "stack up" against others? We need to remember that each of us is called to determine our self-worth in our relationship with our Creator. You are a unique, precious, and irreplaceable daughter of God. If you must indulge the drive to compare yourself to anything, ask God to show you even more clearly the unique plan he has for you. Then stack yourself up against that.

If you answered TRUE to #2, pause for a moment to consider how you might react if your husband dared to say something like, "Doug's wife gets up at the crack of dawn every morning to prepare him a three-course breakfast before he leaves for work. I'm pretty disappointed with these cornflakes."

You might be crushed. Or angry. Or confused. You might be tempted to point out Doug's wife's untidy appearance or ill-behaved children. But one thing is for sure: You would be hurt and feel betrayed by your spouse's unfair comparison. You would be angry at the injustice of your husband stacking up your wifely accomplishments for comparison to another's. And you certainly would not be inspired to rise early the next morning to prepare a gourmet breakfast as a humble gift to your beloved.

When I was a young newlywed, I made the acquaintance of a woman I really thought had lucked out in the husband department. Her man was positively *romantic*. He wrote her poetry for her birthday, always remembered their anniversary in small but meaningful ways, and (here was the part I envied most) he sang his wife's praises every chance he got.

Obviously, she had it made.

Imagine my surprise, then, when I learned years later that this romantic man was romancing someone new. He had abandoned his Catholic Faith, moved out of the home he shared with his wife and three kids, and was pursuing a relationship with a new girlfriend.

Some catch he was.

My point is not that romance is overrated (it is) or that anniversaries are not important (they are), but that we never know another person's interior details completely. The warning about not comparing our own insides to other people's outsides applies to our marriages, too. God gave you your husband—that man sitting in your living room right now—with all his big and small strengths and weaknesses, the ones that only you have the privilege of knowing completely. Your job is to love *that man* well and help him on his way toward heaven. The details of what you think you know about others' relationships are distractions from the very real and very particular calling God has given to you. Focus on loving your husband well, in the ways only you can. Focus on improving yourself as a wife, not on all the ways he does not measure up as a husband. When we pay attention to the details of others' callings and others' relationships, we run the risk of neglecting our own.

If you answered FALSE to #3, you might be tired. Tired of being the only who empties the crumb tray at the bottom of the toaster. Tired of being the only one who can find your son's missing soccer cleat minutes before he has to leave for his game. Tired of being the only one who remembers to send your husband's grandmother flowers for her birthday (and knows what kind she likes).

Can't someone else do all this stuff?

Well, yes and no. It does not take some kind of special skill set to find a cleat or call the florist, but paying attention to all of these small things does require a particular kind of gift a woman excels at.

I once watched my husband struggle to style our youngest daughter's hair into pigtails before leaving for Mass. It was comical. The man was not lacking love or a desire to help, but he had never before attempted little-girl hairstyling and lacked some basic skills. I was usually the one who made sure the girls' hair looked cute for Mass; a mother tends to be the one focused on those kinds of details.

We wear ourselves down when we think of all these little details as drudgery and mind-numbing, meaningless work. Little things do matter—from pretty pigtails to clean bed sheets to birthday cakes frosted with a favorite flavor. We women know this. In our talent for the small things, we find a privilege and a calling, a gift we alone can give to our families.

If you answered FALSE to #4, you need to make a list. Write down all the good things you have ever noticed or that others have ever noticed about your husband and children. Then write a second list of the things that worry, annoy, or embarrass you about your husband and children. Looking at your second list, ask God to speak to your heart about the ways in which he is calling you to grow closer to him through these particular challenges. Looking at your first list, give thanks to God for all the ways he has blessed you through those you love.

If you answered FALSE to #5, pray these words:

Dear God,

Help me to follow Mary's example in serving my family and teaching others to love. Open my eyes to the needs of others, however small, and give me grace to find the means to meet those needs. Thank you for my feminine gift of noticing and valuing even the smallest details. When I am weary from the work of serving my family, remind me of the privilege of loving others as only I can, and strengthen my resolve to use my gifts to bring you glory in all things.

Amen.

Chapter 9

Sensitive Strength

"Respect for the human person proceeds by way of respect for the principle that 'everyone should look upon his neighbor (without any exception) as another self, above all bearing in mind his life and the means necessary for living it with dignity.'"

—Catechism of the Catholic Church *1931*[1]

Strength:
We are sensitive to the
needs of others and stand
up against injustice.

Weakness:
When we focus too much on
"keeping score," we lose sight
of our call to self-giving love.

---

[1] *Gaudium st Spes* 27.

Let's return to the wedding at Cana briefly (see John 2:1-11). Imagine Mary's tone of voice as she spoke those simple words to Jesus.

"They have no wine."

She did not whine, cry, beg, or otherwise cause a scene. She merely stated the facts, describing a problem she had noticed and then trusted that Jesus would be moved to act accordingly.

Even when his first response was seemingly less than agreeable— "Woman, [what does this] have to do with me? My hour has not yet come"—still Mary trusted.

"Do whatever he tells you," she told the servants.

I like to think of this as a defining moment, not only for Christ and the beginning of his public ministry, but for Mary, his mother, and the part she would play—as an example to all women—in the history of salvation.

The fact that Jesus calls his mother "woman" in this passage is significant. By today's standards, it might sound disrespectful. If my teenaged sons ever dare to call me "Woman" instead of "Mother," they will indeed be grounded until their mid-forties. But during Christ's time on earth, "woman" was a term of respect. Christ was recognizing and calling attention to Mary's uniquely feminine role, and addressing her with great dignity and respect. Although the term "woman" may seem off-putting to us at first, it is actually a term associated with Mary's role in salvation history as the "New Eve"—the woman who would crush the head of the serpent.

But what are modern women to make of this scene, and what can Mary's words and actions teach us about the unique value of women and the role we are called to play in society? I think the example Mary sets in this scene points to three special gifts and callings we have as women: We are sensitive to the needs and feelings of others; we stand up for and speak for those who are weak and vulnerable; and we trust the strength of our words to inspire others to action.

We Are Sensitive to Others

As we read in the Gospel, Mary noticed that the wedding hosts were out of wine. She likely knew this would be an embarrassing event on what should have been a joyous occasion. She noticed and was sensitive enough to the needs of others to talk to her son about helping them.

We all do this sort of thing sometimes, don't we? Have you ever kicked your husband under the table at a dinner party when you felt a conversation was going in a bad direction? Have you ever given your children a nudge to be extra kind to a playmate who seems to be having a bad day? Have you ever picked up on a "vibe" about someone's mood or feelings without that person having to verbalize it for you?

We women recognize feelings in others and are sensitive to them in ways that even those in question might not be ready to fully acknowledge. Personally speaking, this "gift" of womanhood is one that causes problems in my marriage periodically.

"What's the matter?" I will ask.

"Nothing," he will answer.

"No, really, what's wrong?"

"Nothing!"

This cycle repeats itself until one of us explodes with frustration or my husband finally feels ready to share some irksome thought that he was not yet comfortable talking about or was not even fully cognizant of at the beginning of our conversation. Sound familiar?

At the wedding at Cana, though, Mary shows us what a gift our sensitivity can be to others. This kind of sensitivity is something sorely lacking in many parts of today's culture, and John Paul II made sure to thank us for it in his letter to women:

> Thank you, *women who are wives!* You irrevocably join your future to that of your husbands, in a relationship of mutual giving, at the service of love and life.

> Thank you, *women who are daughters* and *women who are sisters!* Into the heart of the family, and then of all society, you bring the richness of your sensitivity, your intuitiveness, your generosity and fidelity.[2]

We Speak Out

Mary did not just notice her hosts' problem at the wedding feast, though. She spoke out about it. She knew who had the power to do something to help, and she opened his eyes to the problem. She did not let a little detail like the fact that his "hour had not yet come" stop her. She went to Jesus and presented him with the problem and stayed on the task by directing others to "do whatever he tells you."

2   Letter of Pope John Paul II to Women, 25 June 1995.

We do that, too. In big ways and small ways, women have always been a voice for the vulnerable. We see injustice and we speak out against it. We stand up for the boy down the street who nobody wants to play with because he is "weird." We stand up for the rights of unborn children, abused women, the poor, and the marginalized.

Even in our own homes and families, think of how often we are the voice of mercy and compassion. I know I am. When my husband becomes angry at a child's bad behavior, I am often quick to whisper in his ear some sweet and good thing that child has done recently. Sometimes I even have to squelch this natural inclination, so as not to interfere with the service of justice. Softhearted mothers everywhere are quick to forgive and move on, perhaps even before their children have learned a proper lesson. But that is one reason God gave them a mother *and* a father. Generally speaking, women are the voice of mercy through love, and men are the voice of mercy through justice. Together, we represent both sides of our loving God; we balance each other out.

But one of the unique abilities of women is to speak for others who are needy and vulnerable. Think of the women who followed Christ along the steps of his passion. Think of Mary who, in her apparitions, speaks words of mercy, compassion, and love to even the worst of sinners. Mary's role has always been one of intercession. Woman's role has always been one of intercession as well. We notice the needs of others, witness injustice, and speak out on behalf of those who need help.

We Trust in the Goodness of Others

At Cana, Mary did not tell Jesus how to handle the situation. She did not suggest turning water into wine. She knew that only Christ had the power to address the situation, and she brought the need of others to him. After that, she trusted.

She trusted that her words would be enough to move him.

She trusted that he would know what needed to be done and would make right decisions about how to address the situation.

She trusted that he had the power to do whatever needed to be done. "Do whatever he tells you," she told the servants.

She did not say, "Why doesn't everyone gather some water, and then let's see what he can do with it. Jesus? Do you think you can work with water, or should we get something else for you? Grape juice, maybe? Would you prefer to work directly with the jars, or maybe you'd like to make some miracle money so we can buy more wine? Or could you arrange a wine delivery?"

No. She just trusted. She trusted that her words would be enough to move the proper people into action, including the God-made-Man, who happened to be her son.

This is good news for all of us would-be control freaks running around noticing everyone's needs and feelings and wondering how on earth we are going to manage to take care of them all. We do not have to take care of it all. We can speak out and then trust; we can pray and then trust, especially in situations that are beyond our control.

Scorekeepers Always Lose

So what are these situations that are beyond our control, where we need to let go and trust? It might be figuring out how you are going to afford to send your kids to college. It might be trying to reach the heart of a pregnant teen with a message of hope and life. It might be navigating a minefield of in-law relationships at the Thanksgiving dinner table. Or ... it might just be figuring out why you are the only person in your entire house who can replace the toilet paper roll in the bathroom.

Have we talked lately about the toilet paper roll? About how I am always the one who puts on a new roll when the old one runs out? Really, I am. Are you also blessed with this honor at your house?

You see, when it comes to TP patrol, I am a scorekeeper. And if you read the heading at the beginning of this section, you already know: Scorekeepers always lose.

It is just human nature to count our own costs in excruciating detail, while failing to fully appreciate the contributions of others. In other words, I am not likely to notice when my husband or one of the children replaces a roll of toilet paper. (But, really, they don't. No one does it but me!) But I do notice (and maybe huff and puff and roll my eyes a little) each and every precious time I enter a bathroom that is out of toilet paper. I notice the 4.6 seconds I must spend removing the empty roll and replacing it with a new one because I. Am. The. Only. One. Who *ever* does a blessed thing around here.

If ever we ran out of toilet paper while I was out of town, I am convinced that my husband and children would go without toilet paper for days until my return. Or maybe they would call my mother. I am pretty sure she is the source of my TP skills.

Trusting Takes Practice

I do not have a magic solution for all of us hopeless scorekeepers, but I can tell you that a bitter and angry habit of scorekeeping when it comes to household chores ("Whose turn is it to take out the trash?") or your marriage ("I always remember our anniversary— Why can't he remember, too?") or your friendships ("Why do I always have to be the one to call her first?") leads to misery. Letting go of scorekeeping and learning to trust God and others who love you can be very liberating.

I am not saying we cannot address injustices, but I am saying that after we have spoken out about our concerns and others have responded (however inadequate we might deem their response to be), there comes a time when we need to make peace with our situation and turn it over to God.

St. John Vianney reminds us: "God commands you to pray, but forbids you to worry."

Sometimes God answers our prayers and meets our needs in ways we could never have imagined—through other people to whom he has given the responsibility. Nothing has taught me this lesson of trust more surely than marriage and motherhood. I have learned to trust priests' advice in the confessional during times when I was confused. I have learned to trust doctors to care for my children and myself when we needed medical attention. And I have learned that dependence upon my husband for my own physical needs and for those of our children is an ongoing lesson in trust. My husband and I may sometimes disagree about the details, but I must admit that when I have been willing to simply trust him, he has come through in ways that have surprised me.

It was a cool fall day ten years ago when Dan pulled our banged-up Volvo station wagon to the side of a country road and waved his hand toward the nearby woods.

"This is it!" he beamed.

I looked. I saw trees.

"Here?" I questioned him. "Right here?"

He pointed to a "For Sale" sign stapled to a tree and nodded.

I pulled my rather pregnant self out of the front seat, unbuckled the seat belts of four-year-old Kateri, three-year-old Eamon, and baby Ambrose in the backseat, and, with Ambrose in my arms, marched boldly into the woods.

There was no path. A gold-and-crimson carpet of fallen leaves crunched underfoot. Dan went ahead, pointing out uneven spots and holding branches out of the way for his lumbering wife and toddling preschoolers.

After a short while, he stopped and we stood beside him. I looked back but could no longer see the road. Trees and heavy branches were thick in all directions.

Dan knelt on the ground before us and brushed aside some leaves, revealing a patch of bare soil. It was only then that I noticed he had brought along a shovel. It cut into the earth as Dan turned over the soil. He pushed the shovel into the earth again, and Eamon squatted beside him, watching. As he dug, dappled sunlight filtered through the autumn leaves and danced on the baby's face as he slept in my arms.

After several more shovelfuls, Dan knelt to scoop soil from the hole and then filled a small plastic cup from a soil test kit. He tightened its lid and looked around with satisfaction.

I still saw trees. But he saw something more.

The soil test was just the beginning. In the following weeks and months, trees were cleared, a well was dug, and a frame was put in place for a foundation. The day we were scheduled for a concrete delivery, Dan gathered medals of our favorite saints—Mary, Joseph, Michael, Kateri, and Anne. These he placed in the corners before the concrete was poured. Our home would be built upon tangible bits of our faith. Our heavenly friends were here for good, and so were we.

When I was a girl and thought of being married and having a house one day, I imagined it would be the kind of house I grew up in—a split-entry ranch in the suburbs with a manicured yard and a swing set. I loved my house growing up. I still do.

I never imagined that when I had a home of my own, it would be because we cut through a thick patch of wilderness to build it. I never thought that I would live in a house where every square inch was planned and put into place by my husband's own calloused hands. I could not have known that I would watch Dan spend years cutting wood, framing walls, and sanding floors to shape this small patch of earth into the vision he saw that day in the woods.

Those early days of making plans for our home highlight for me a difference between the kinds of roles we are called to as men and as women. John Paul II referred our feminine strengths and gifts as our "feminine genius," but there is such thing as a "masculine genius" as well.

While women are more naturally inclined to notice and care about details, most men have a gift for seeing the "bigger picture" in a way that can be hard for us to understand. I stood in the woods that day and saw only trees, but Dan had a grand vision for our future home—a vision I did not share, but one he knew he could turn into reality. God made men and women for different purposes; our gifts and strengths are complementary, and together, we serve our families, our communities, and our Church in very different ways. The *Catechism* clarifies this.

> Man and woman were made "for each other"—not that God left them half-made and incomplete: he created them to be a communion of persons, in which each can be a "helpmate" to the other, for they are equal as persons ("bone of my bones ...") and complementary as masculine and feminine.[3]

It is in embracing our sexual differences and our complementarity that men and women find fulfillment in the roles God intends for them to play. We are made for communion with one another and, ultimately, union with God. In recognizing our natural feminine strengths and appreciating the ways in which masculine traits "complete" them, we can find joy and satisfaction in our family lives, in our workplaces, and in our communities.

John Paul II recognized this call to communion and the human longing for the kind of unity that can only come from self-giving love.

> In the "unity of the two," man and woman are called from the beginning not only to exist "side by side" or "together," but

---

[3]   *Catechism of the Catholic Church* 372; Genesis 2:24.

they are also called *to exist mutually "one for the other."* ... To be human means to be called to interpersonal communion *[communio personarum]*. ... Being a person means striving towards self-realization, which can only be achieved *through a "sincere gift of self."*[4]

The "sincere gift of self" John Paul II talks about is a lifetime calling. It is a challenge that most of us will rise to, fall short of, and strive toward again and again, as we grow together in our marriages and family lives.

Late one night, after the kids were asleep, Dan and I were awake in our bedroom. Cool night air rushed in through screened windows as we lay in the dark, talking, laughing, and at last falling silent, waiting for sleep. Darkness hung thick in the woods around us. As I do each night, I thought of each child asleep in his or her bed and asked God to watch over and fill each of them with his grace.

I thought too of the spot in the woods where Dan cut into the earth on that autumn afternoon long ago. I know now that Dan's vision in the woods was only a little bit about the house. Here inside these walls is something more precious than that. These small souls we are raising, and this family we are building, are a bigger dream still. A house is just a house. But home is wherever we are. All of us, together.

---

[4]   *Mulieris Dignitatem* 7.

Are You Mary at the Feast?

Answer TRUE or FALSE to the following:

_____ 1. I appreciate and cultivate my ability to be sensitive to the needs and feelings of others.

_____ 2. I am unafraid to stand up and speak out against injustice when I see it.

_____ 3. I can list the last five household tasks I did and the last five tasks my husband did (or did not) do.

_____ 4. I trust that God loves me and will care for me, especially through other people in my life.

_____ 5. I frequently worry so much that I have trouble sleeping at night.

If you answered FALSE to #1, ask the Holy Spirit to inspire you with the thought of someone who could use some extra help or attention right now. It might be your husband or one of your children who is having a bad day. It might be a neighbor who could use a break and some help with childcare. It might be a relative who needs a phone call ... just because.

Recall a time when you were particularly touched by another woman's thoughtfulness. What was it that you noticed and appreciated most? Was it the details of the words or actions themselves or the thoughts behind them? Give thanks to God for that person's generosity, and ask him to inspire the same womanly virtue in you.

If you answered FALSE to #2, consider what might be holding you back from speaking out against things you know are wrong. Is it the fear of standing out or being different? Is it an aversion to conflict? Is it laziness? Whatever it is, spend some time reflecting on the meaning of this familiar passage:

> You are the salt of the earth; but if salt has lost its taste, how shall its saltness be restored? It is no longer good for anything except to be thrown out and trodden under foot by men. You are the light of the world. A city set on a hill cannot be hid. Nor do men light a lamp and put it under a bushel, but on a stand, and it gives light to all in the house. Let your light so shine before men, that they may see your good works and give glory to your Father who is in heaven. (Matthew 5:13-16).

As an introvert, I completely understand where you are coming from. Nothing about being a "city set on a mountain" sounds even a little bit comfortable to me. I break out in hives every time I read this passage and wonder if I cannot just do the whole "salt of the earth" thing from behind a computer screen with a pen name. I would rather not be the "holy roller" who spoils everyone's fun when a conversation among women turns gossipy or when the parish pro-life group invites me to hold a sign in front of an abortion clinic. Sometimes, when an acquaintance pronounces the Catholic Church's position on same-sex marriage an "abomination," I think sitting in front of a computer is about as much "light" as I can handle.

The good news is that, while we all are called to be a voice of mercy and love for those who have no voice, the details of that calling are different for everyone. I thank God for the essential work women like Abby Johnson, Lila Rose, Janet Smith, and Helen Alvaré do for the pro-life cause, but I also thank God that he has called me to a different kind of pro-life witness—every bit as essential, but perhaps in a smaller, less spotlighted way.

If you answered TRUE to #3, you are definitely a scorekeeper. And you lose. Really. You will wind up resentful and bitter—I guarantee it. It is hard to stop keeping score, though, isn't it? Here is something that helped me quit some of my scorekeeping habits. If you are going to keep score, set a goal of making the score come out uneven in other people's favor. It might sound crazy, but for me it really works.

You can still keep track of who does what around the house, but you only "win" this game if you are doing the most. Make sure you are always the last person who took out the trash, the first person to jump up and do the dishes, and the person who feeds the dog the most often. You might think this is horribly unfair and unwise— you will become a doormat, after all.

No, you will not. Just try it. Any woman who is a scorekeeper at heart needs this kind of check to offset her own unbalanced tendencies. I know this because I have been there myself. Give the worries about "justice" to God, and let him figure out all those details. You will have peace of heart to show for it in the end, and isn't that what really matters?

If you answered FALSE to #4, you may need to practice letting go. God gave you the gift of noticing details and needs, but he does not always provide you with the means of attending to those details and needs by yourself. Think of Mary's trusting example: "Do whatever he tells you." Ask her to help you follow that example in meaningful ways in your life.

The next time you find yourself turning to God for some need, say your prayer of petition, but also ask for the grace of letting go of that concern. Place your concern in the hands of God, and then get back to your own work and duties. Keep your eyes open to the ways in which God might inspire others in your life to meet your needs in unexpected ways.

Do you trust your husband to love you and take care of your needs? For example, if he is the main provider for your family, do you worry excessively about bills and financial problems that are his responsibility? Give him the gift of your trust and confidence in his abilities, and he might just surprise you with his renewed spirit of generosity and capability.

If you answered TRUE to #5, memorize this prayer, from St. Teresa of Avila:

"Let nothing disturb you,
Let nothing frighten you,
All things are passing away:
God never changes.
Patience obtains all things.
Whoever has God lacks nothing;
God alone suffices."

The next time you find yourself awake at
night and worrying, pray this prayer or
some other short aspiration
(i.e., "Jesus, I place my trust in you!"), and
focus on resting in the loving arms of
Jesus until you fall asleep.

Chapter 10

We Need Each Other

"Friendship, as has been said, consists in a full commitment of the will to another person with a view to that person's good."

—St. John Paul II[1]

Recently, an older lady approached me in the parking lot as I was walking into Mass.

"Can you help me out with something, woman to woman?" she asked.

"Of course," I replied.

She felt something bothering her in the back of her blouse, she explained, and could not quite reach the spot to find out what it was. She turned around and pointed to the spot. I reached in and pulled out ... a hair roller. The two of us stood together in the church parking lot, looked at the pink foam roller in my hand, and laughed out loud.

---

[1] Karol Wojtyla, *Love and Responsibility* (San Francisco: Ignatius Press, 1993), 92.

I think this silly story is a good illustration of the kind of encouragement and support every one of us needs. We need someone who can reach where we cannot, show us the truth about what bothers us most, and then join us as we laugh at the joyful absurdity of it all, woman to woman.

I sent a text message to a friend recently. It *might* have been just a little whiny and complaining about my horrific life and all the annoying ways in which my sorry excuse for a family fails to appreciate me.

I cannot be sure.

But even if it was a tad on the whiny side, my friend's reply snapped me right out of it. It was equal parts compassion ("Oh, I hate when that happens! I'm so sorry!") *and* a call to be my better self ("Maybe next time you can say how you feel and then not get quite so emotional? Walk away and do something fun to distract yourself?")

It was exactly what I needed to hear. I think it is exactly what every one of us needs to hear when we are struggling: compassion without wallowing and challenge without judgment. No one can say these things to a woman quite like another woman can, whether it is your mom, your sister, a girlfriend, or even that random lady you run into in the department-store dressing room.

We need each other. We really do. Do you believe that? We do.

Years ago, I was standing in line at the pharmacy with my then-four-year-old son when he began a predictable whine-fest for gum.

"No gum today," I told him. But the line was long, and he was persistent. He threw his small body to the floor and pulled at my pant legs.

"Want guuuuu-uuuuum," he argued convincingly.

A tantrum was starting to swell. I did a quick cost-benefit analysis and decided to cut my losses—I handed the child a package of gum. As I did so, however, I heard a loud sigh behind me and turned around in time to see a young woman rolling her eyes at her companion.

I knew what she was thinking: *If you reward whiny, demanding behavior with a package of gum, how on earth can you expect a four-year-old to learn not to be whiny and demanding?*

I knew her thoughts with clarity, you see, because I used to *be* that woman—smug, unmarried, well-groomed, a future perfect parent. In the pharmacy, however, I was not perfect. I was only embarrassed. I spared the disapproving woman my true thoughts, but I might have explained to her that most of my family was suffering from strep throat and desperately needed the lozenges, Tylenol, and coloring books I was waiting to purchase. I might have told her that this particular boy, though we love him ferociously, has always been an exceptionally needy and volatile child. I might have told her that while we were working on correcting certain behaviors with him, "Don't beg for gum in line at the pharmacy" had not made the short list. We were focusing instead on, "Don't throw glass" and, "Don't hit the baby."

My exasperation in the pharmacy that day was relieved, however, by a different woman—one who responded to my plight with support instead of superiority.

"He's a tough kid," an older woman said, smiling in my direction. "That kind of grit will take him places."

I smiled back.

And that was all I needed. I was renewed. I was empowered. I was a positive parenting force once again. Bring it on, darling child. Bring it on.

While it is true that no one can tear apart a vulnerable woman quite like another woman can, it is equally true that no one can build up and encourage a vulnerable woman quite like another woman can. We cannot ever truly know another's interior plight and particular challenges. It is important to stand up for the truth, and there is a place for admonishing the sinner, but that never means using others' weaknesses and vulnerabilities to feed our own egos.

These days, I ask God to help me become more affirming like the second woman at the pharmacy and less critical like the first. Because, truth be told, we are all a little of both. Valiant women of faith are a great gift to each other, but only if we allow ourselves to be, only if we remain receptive to one another and reject the temptation to compare, judge, and draw lines of division between our sisters and ourselves.

Mom Is Enough

We women need to unite with our sisters in arms because, whether we realize it or not, we are engaged in a great battle. Against sexism.

Wait a minute, you might be thinking. *We live in an enlightened age. Does sexism against women even exist anymore?*

I think it does.

We certainly (and thankfully) see relatively few incidents of *Mad Men*-style remarks or behind-slapping in office settings these days. I would argue, though, that a different kind of sexism is alive and well today. It is a sexism that, ironically, many of us have embraced with the intention of liberating women from stereotypes and limitations; it is a sexism that devalues women by devaluing motherhood.

I see sexism in words written online, where men and women alike dismiss an entire class of female writers with a single derisive term: *"mommy blogger."* Even in Christian circles, context and tone sometimes turn "mommy" into a sneer, a put-down, a condescending label.

I hear sexism when I read the words that a talented and intelligent colleague of mine once wrote: "I'm not just a mom. There is more to me than that. I am not defined by my motherhood."

Do women need to do and be more than the very purpose for which God created them? I do not necessarily mean the production and care of genetic offspring. I mean not *what* God made us (spouse, parent, nun, sister, friend, daughter, worker, volunteer), but *who* God made us: Women. Life-givers. Nurturers. Encouragers. Peacemakers. Teachers. Mothers. Are these things so trivial and meaningless that we need to prove we are "more" than them?

I will be the first unenlightened, politically incorrect "Neanderthal" naive enough to say: "I am just a mom. And not only am I "just a mom," but I am "just a mom" to each of my unique children in a unique way, just for them. I am proud to be a life-giving nurturer and a feminine influence in my marriage, my home, my family, and my community, and the all-encompassing word "mother" absolutely is "all" that I am. Every day I pray for the grace to do this "just a mom" thing well. Because *that* would be enough.

When I was young, I used to wonder and worry about what my life would be like and who I might be someday. I used to fret that I might make the wrong decision or fail to make the right one and mess up God's plan for me. But I am beginning to know better than that. We do not change who we are with the decisions we make. We can sin, but sin does change us in terrible ways; God's plan for our lives and his will for us, however, is unchangingly written in our very hearts and souls. We cannot mess that up; we can only hurt ourselves by trying to deny it or failing to recognize its worth.

One night, my youngest son, seven-year-old Daniel, woke from a nightmare and claimed his place in my arms for a few precious minutes. As I held him close in the dark, I recalled the time years ago, when he was a very small baby.

I need you, Mama, his reaching arms would say to me. *And I need you, Baby,* my arms would reach right back. A baby needs warmth and love, milk and kisses, every bit as much as a mother longs to give him those things. We are called to this kind of intimate communion with others and in a special way to the human beings— whether they are our children, husbands, parents, siblings, students, patients, friends, neighbors, or co-workers—that God places in our care. The details might vary and change, but the call to self-giving love never does.

That late night, when my growing "baby" Daniel let me know he was ready to go back to his bed, I carried him upstairs and tucked him in. When I kissed him good night, though, I paused. Because there, in that one small moment, hanging in the air between his small, shining face and mine, I felt the grace of knowing who I am.

Mom. Mother. Mama. Me.

I am not "just" somebody's mom, but *this* little boy's mom. Daniel's mom. I am the body that keeps him warm, the arms that hold him close, the cheek that presses against his and makes him feel wanted, known, and loved. That privileged person is me; that privileged place is mine; and nothing else matters in that small but essential space. Right here is all that God made me to be—mother. Danny's mom, me.

Woman to Woman

Women have a special capacity for fostering feminine strengths in one another. Only together can we fully recognize and rejoice in our momnipotence—our power and strength to change the world through our feminine genius, our universal motherhood. Together, we women can affirm and build up our God-given feminine gifts of sensitivity, gentleness, and nurturing love. Together, women become more perfectly the gift to the world that God made us to be.

Do you know momnipotent women? Do they know just how momnipotent they are? What joys might we find in using our own feminine gifts to celebrate and encourage those same strengths in others?

What kind of world would it be if every woman embraced the all-encompassing, all-powerful role of "mother" and gave that calling the respect it deserves? What might happen if every one of us fully recognized and celebrated her God-given, momnipotent gifts and the potential she has to change the world for the better? What kind of happiness and satisfaction might we find in our universal call to motherhood—biological, adoptive, and spiritual—if we gave glory to God by using our feminine strengths to build up his kingdom on earth?

Are you ready? Let's find out.

The time has come for you to use your momnipotence to make the world a better place. The good news is that you can start right now, in your own home, even as stuffed animals fly through the air and a naked toddler streaks through the living room. And the better news is that in doing so, you will find peace, balance, and joy in the role God gave you:

Mom. Mother. Mama. You.